3-MINUTE
DEVOTIONS
for an
Anxious Heart

3-MINUTE DEVOTIONS

for an
Anxious Heart

180 Readings for a Peaceful Spirit

LINDA HANG

BARBOUR
PUBLISHING

Print ISBN 978-1-63609-166-2

Published by Barbour Publishing, Inc., 1810 Barbour Drive, Uhrichsville, Ohio 44683, www.barbourbooks.com

Our mission is to inspire the world with the life-changing message of the Bible.

ecpa Member of the
Evangelical Christian
Publishers Association

Introduction

Looking for a moment or two of peace and encouragement for your anxious heart?

Here is a collection of moments from the true source of all peace and encouragement—God's Word. In these pages you'll be guided through just-right-sized readings designed to fit into the busiest, most restless days—even if you only have three minutes.

Minute 1: Reflect on God's Word.
Minute 2: Read real-life application
and encouragement.
Minute 3: Pray.

These devotions aren't meant to be a replacement for digging deep into the scriptures or for personal, in-depth quiet time. Instead, consider them a perfect jump-start as you form a habit of spending time with God every day. Add them to the time you're already spending with Him. Or pick one to read on a day when you need a little extra peace in your heart.

Then share these moments with others who need some peace and encouragement too.

*Your word is a lamp to guide
my feet and a light for my path.*

PSALM 119:105 NLT

Do Not Worry

"I tell you this: Do not worry about your life."
MATTHEW 6:25 NLV

Jesus said, *"Do not worry."* In other words, do not fret, do not dread—do not be anxious. Sounds simple enough.

"Yeah," we might counter, "but what about violence where we once were safe?"

"Do not worry."

"What about invisible threats like diseases?"

"Do not worry."

"What about economic crashes?"

"Do not worry."

"What about the endless everyday problems?"

"Do not worry."

"What about. . . ?"

"Do not worry."

How is not worrying possible in a world brimming with reasons to worry? Only with God's help. . .the One who sees every worrisome thing eons before it happens. . .the One who plans *and* brings about good from the bad. . .the One who holds our lives—lives that we are so anxious about—securely in His hands.

Lord, teach me how to follow Your words. Transform my anxious heart into a heart that does not worry. Amen.

All the Day Long

Evening, morning and noon I cry out
in distress, and he hears my voice.
PSALM 55:17 NIV

When do worries show up? Just in the morning? Only when we turn out the lights to sleep? No. Worries happen all day, and they can appear out of nowhere. . .while we're commuting to work, while we're nuking our lunch, while we're folding laundry, while we're snuggled on the sofa watching our favorite show—bam! Our hearts become anxious over something.

The psalmist wrote that he cried out to God throughout the day. What about us? We don't have to confine our prayers to morning or bedtime devotions. We can cry out to God with our worries whenever they surface, no matter how often. In fact, the more regularly we talk to God, the less anxious our hearts will be.

Lord, morning, noon, and night—all day long—
I pray to You. Thank You for caring enough to listen
as I let You know what's troubling me. Amen.

When the Time Comes

*"God will help you deal with whatever hard
things come up when the time comes."*
MATTHEW 6:34 MSG

What is it about worrying that makes us think it helps?
Worrying about job security won't prevent layoffs. Worrying
over the car breaking down won't stop the car from breaking
down. Worrying whether a relationship will turn sour won't
keep it sweet. Worrying if we'll get cancer won't boost our
health. Worrying about anything won't help.

But there is something that will help: focusing on the
Someone who helps us. As humans, we anticipate lots of hard
things happening, even though lots of those hard things may
never happen. God, on the other hand, doesn't guess—He
knows exactly when we'll need help, and He promises to get
us through those moments. Don't be anxious about tomorrow's
what-ifs. God has already got that covered.

---

*What a relief, Lord! I can put my anxious
thoughts out of my mind, resting instead
in the certainty that You will help. Amen.*

Just a Worrywart?

"If your eye is the reason you fall into sin, take it out."
MARK 9:47 NLV

When Jesus taught His followers how to handle sin, He didn't mince words. He used an image that made God's teachings plain: take sin seriously; deal with it drastically.

What does that have to do with our anxious hearts? We all experience unease. We all face situations that cause worry. It's what we do with those anxious thoughts that matters. If we hold on to them, choosing not to trust God, it is sin. And Jesus' remedy for sin isn't to coddle it or to gloss over it.

If you'd describe yourself as a habitual worrier, follow Jesus' words. Ask His help in identifying the areas that cause you to stumble. Then be ready to make changes.

Lord, when I worry over and over, I'm telling You that I don't trust You. Forgive me. Show me where and how to trust You more and more. Amen.

Anxious Objector

But Moses said, "Pardon your servant,
Lord. Please send someone else."

EXODUS 4:13 NIV

Moses was tending sheep when something peculiar happened. He saw a bush with flames inside, yet the bush did not burn. Naturally, Moses went to investigate. As he drew near, God spoke to him and commissioned him to rescue the Israelites from Egypt. God assured Moses that He would go with him. He even demonstrated signs that would prove to the people that He had sent Moses. But Moses began to fret—like many of us would have done in his shoes. He got hung up on the fact that he was no public speaker.

Despite Moses' request to spare him, God didn't send a substitute. He was about to teach Moses, and us, an important lesson: when we are completely incapable, God is completely capable.

Lord, my life is heading in a direction that makes
me anxious. Remind me that if You will it, it
will be You who sees me through. Amen.

All Good

*And we know that for those who love
God all things work together for good.*
ROMANS 8:28 ESV

Some situations don't end the way we want them to. No matter how hard we pray, sometimes bad things happen. Can we *not* be anxious when we're facing a possible worst-case scenario?

Only if we view our lives through the promise of Romans 8:28: "We know that for those who love God all things work together for good." Notice: It's not just some things, the things that aren't *too* bad, that work together for good. All things work together for good. How? Because God is behind the good. He is the driving force: "We know that God *makes* all things work together for the good of those who love Him" (NLV, italics added).

Do you love God? Be at peace. He's working for your good.

---

*Lord, I don't understand what good can come
from this bad, but I'm trusting You to make things
good in Your own way and time. Amen.*

Though the Earth

God is our refuge and strength, an ever-present help in trouble. Therefore we will not fear, though the earth give way and the mountains fall into the heart of the sea.

PSALM 46:1–2 NIV

Psalm 46:2 describes a scene fit for a Hollywood movie: the earth crumbling, entire mountains crashing into the sea. If we witnessed that event for real, we'd be terrified. Yes? But the psalmist declared that even then there's no need to fear. His confidence hinges on the truth of the first verse, that God is a safe place for us, His help always available. *Therefore* nothing can cause us to fear for long.

In your most anxious moments, turn to God, who says to His people, "Though the mountains be shaken and the hills be removed, yet my unfailing love for you will not be shaken nor my covenant of peace be removed" (Isaiah 54:10 NIV).

Lord, when there's trouble in front of me, I'll turn around—and find myself in Your embrace. Amen.

Things Above

Keep your minds thinking about things in heaven.
Do not think about things on the earth.
<small>COLOSSIANS 3:2 NLV</small>

French philosopher René Descartes is famous for the saying "I think, therefore I am." We could also say we are what we think about.

If our thoughts center on the things that make us anxious, we will be anxious. But if our thoughts center on our source of peace, we will be peaceful. That's one reason Paul wrote, "Set your minds on things above, not on earthly things" (Colossians 3:2 NIV). If our minds dwell on earth, so will our hearts. If our minds dwell in heaven, our hearts will soon follow. Now, obviously we can't *only* think of heaven and our future there. Bills need to be paid, kids need to be fed, leaking pipes need to be fixed. . . . Yet imagine what a difference it would make if our thoughts kept circling back to things above!

Lord, so often my mind is stuck in my concerns.
Help me lift my thoughts to You. Amen.

The Savior's Response

Then Jesus went with his disciples to a place called Gethsemane. . . . And he began to be sorrowful and troubled.
MATTHEW 26:36–37 NIV

Jesus knew He would be crucified soon. Had He dreaded this time before He reached Gethsemane? Had He felt the pangs of what was coming for weeks or months? Maybe not. But when He stepped foot in the garden, He was troubled.

So what did the Son of God do in response to His unsettled soul? He didn't pace. He didn't sit then fidget then nervously sit somewhere else. "Going a little farther, he fell with his face to the ground and prayed" (Matthew 26:39 NIV). Our anxious times may not be as extreme as what Jesus faced, but our response can be the same. We can step away and tell our Father how we feel.

Lord, my prayers won't always change the situation, but they will always change the state of my heart. May I have Your peace no matter what lies ahead. Amen.

Inconceivable Peace

*And the peace of God, which surpasses
all understanding, will guard your hearts
and your minds in Christ Jesus.*

PHILIPPIANS 4:7 ESV

A little anxiety requires a little peace. But what if your worry is a hulking beast of a worry? Or what if you worry about *everything*? Great anxiety requires great peace.

Think that kind of peace doesn't exist? At times, having great peace may be inconceivable; always, it's humanly impossible. For great peace, we must go to the Prince of Peace. "The peace of God is much greater than the human mind can understand. This peace will keep your hearts and minds through Christ Jesus" (Philippians 4:7 NLV). The Christian who relies on God can face the most angst-ridden circumstances and be at peace. Those of the world will shake their heads in disbelief. But although God's peace is inconceivable, it's real nonetheless.

---

*Lord, peace seems impossible right now. As I
come to You with my worries, releasing them
to You, please fill me with Your peace. Amen.*

Perfect Peace

*"You keep him in perfect peace whose mind
is stayed on you, because he trusts in you."*
ISAIAH 26:3 ESV

Blame it on too-busy schedules. Blame it on overstimulation from dozens of screens. Blame it on whatever you want to, but the fact remains: our minds can be flighty. Something is always commandeering our thoughts, and we're left frazzled, stressed, anxious.

God offers the opposite. He stands in readiness to keep us in perfect peace—complete, lasting, blessed peace. To experience that peace, we first have to train our minds to stay grounded on the firm foundation of our God. God is trustworthy through thick and thin, but how can we trust One to whom we are only casually devoted, One who enters our thoughts only once or twice a day? With minds stayed on Him, though, we are sure of Him—and kept in perfect peace.

---

*Lord, the more I think about You, the more I trust You,
and that's when peace is perfected in me! Amen.*

Out-of-This-World Peace

"Peace I leave with you; my peace I give to you. Not as the world gives do I give to you. Let not your hearts be troubled."

JOHN 14:27 ESV

Need to dial down your anxiety? There's an app for that. Want to be calmer? Take a supplement. Our world has a lot of solutions for anxious hearts, but not one of them yields the peace we crave. How can soul-deep peace—a peace that will withstand our chaotic life—come out of a world that is so broken? We aim for peace. We often miss. We create peace. We only touch the surface.

Jesus left the chaos behind after His resurrection, but He also left His peace. Not the hit-or-miss, surface-level peace of our world. A peace you can stake your life on. A peace that's through and through. A peace that is ours.

Lord, You don't want my heart to be troubled; You want me to have peace. Thank You for providing what I never could. Amen.

The Rock

*From the end of the earth will I cry unto
thee, when my heart is overwhelmed: lead
me to the rock that is higher than I.*

PSALM 61:2 KJV

Ever feel that anxiety is lapping at your chin? That just one
more worry will cause those churning waters to rise above
your head? What do you do then?

King David experienced trying times throughout his
life. Psalm 61 may have been written while his son Absalom
attempted to oust him from the throne. But as the waters of
trouble began rising, David did what David did best: He called
to his God. He sought relief in the One who was higher than
he was—higher than his problems too.

Whenever your heart is overwhelmed—your anxiety
rising, just about to engulf you—cry out to God. Let your
prayers lead you to the Rock. Let Him lift you high above
the troubles.

---

*Lord, I cry to You in my anxiety. Pull me
into the refuge of Your presence. Amen.*

The One Thing

"Martha, Martha, you are worried and troubled about many things. Only a few things are important, even just one. Mary has chosen the good thing. It will not be taken away from her."

LUKE 10:41–42 NLV

Martha: *My feet are killing me! Sure wish I could just sit down—like Mary. But what about supper? Who will set the table, cook those vegetables— Oh, the bread is burning! Maybe later I'll be able to sit and listen, after supper's cleaned up and Lazarus's tunic is mended and. . .*

Can you relate? Of course, we don't know Martha's actual thoughts. Luke only records that she vented her frustration to Jesus. What's key is Jesus' gentle reply to Martha, one we would do well to hear ourselves: we will never run out of things to fuss over. So will we choose to focus on the one thing that matters most?

Lord, spending time with You is not a waste. Help me set aside distractions and sit awhile with You. Amen.

Do Not

"Therefore I tell you, do not worry."

LUKE 12:22 NIV

Dozens of times throughout scripture, you'll find verses about not worrying or being anxious. If you lined them up, you'd notice a pattern. They're not suggestions. They're imperatives. They're commands. "Do not worry." "Do not be troubled." "Do not be anxious."

Now, God is a loving God. All that He commands teaches us how to live the best life. And the best life begins inside—with the condition of our hearts. The psalmist said, "Search me, O God, and know my heart! . . . See if there be any grievous way in me" (Psalm 139:23-24 ESV). He realized that no one could live the best life with pride or hate, greed or lust inhabiting their heart. Ditto for anxiety.

God has told us, "Do not be anxious." Through Him, let us obey.

Lord, You say not to worry, and because You are with me, I can do just that. Help my life be pleasing to You in every way. Amen.

Great News!

"In this world you will have trouble. But take heart! I have overcome the world."

JOHN 16:33 NIV

"I have good news and I have bad news—which do you want first?" Does anyone welcome those words? Jesus didn't preface His good news-bad news statement. He just said it.

So let's start with the bad news: "In this world you will have trouble." Maybe, as Christians, we'd like to hear something else—some promise of a charmed life—but the bad news shouldn't come as a shock. We don't have to live long before we're well acquainted with the troubles of this world.

Now for the good news: "But take heart! I have overcome the world." There's trouble ahead, yes, but God has paved a way through it. *No* trouble is any match for God. And that's not just good news. That's great news.

---

*Lord, You warn us; You also make a promise.
You have told us these things so that in
You we may have peace! Amen.*

The Lord's Servants

"I am the Lord's servant," Mary answered.
"May your word to me be fulfilled."
LUKE 1:38 NIV

Think about Mary. Are you envisioning the angel Gabriel's visit? Are you remembering Mary's later words of praise, known to us as the Magnificat? From there you might skip to the manger, the twinkling-stars night when Peace came to earth. But what about the nine months in between Gabriel's visit and Jesus' birth? What was it like for Mary, a first-time expectant mom, the talk of the town? Was Mary anxious as she faced the days ahead?

If Mary's humble response to God's call is any indication, she likely continued to offer herself to God day by day by day. As we face surprising, challenging circumstances, sometimes all we can do is put ourselves into the Master's hands, trusting His will for our lives. But as we do that one thing, we will be upheld by His peace too.

Lord, here I am, Your servant. May
Your Word be fulfilled in my life. Amen.

Casting Anxiety

Cast all your anxiety on him because he cares for you.
1 PETER 5:7 NIV

Why do we worry? Maybe the act of worrying gives us a sense of control. If a problem is in our minds, then it's not out of our hands.

Except, somewhere inside, we all know that isn't true. We all know that worrying doesn't achieve much but a knotted stomach. Jesus put it this way: "Which of you by being anxious can add a single hour to his span of life?" (Matthew 6:27 ESV).

It's okay to let go of your worries and give them to God. The Bible tells us to cast our anxiety on Him. Imagine trekking down a road, your back burdened with a heavy weight, then hefting the load off your back. What relief—to stand straight, to walk unburdened.

So go ahead: unload on God. That's exactly what He wants from you.

Lord, thank You that I don't need to hang on to my worries. I leave them in Your care. Amen.

Each Time

What time I am afraid, I will trust in thee. In God
I will praise his word, in God I have put my trust.
PSALM 56:3–4 KJV

A worry that's allowed to stew will expand. Maybe you've experienced that phenomenon yourself. One worry enters your mind. You think about it a little then try to push it aside, but it keeps coming back. Each time the worry returns, you think on it longer and longer. Pretty soon it's all that fills your mind. Meanwhile, anxiety fills your heart.

What's the alternative? At the first hint of worry, pray. Seek out God and talk to Him honestly. Each time worry returns, renew your trust in the One who is absolutely trustworthy. Pretty soon praise will fill your mind and peace will fill your heart.

Lord, You already know this thought that's making me
anxious. I'm not waiting; I'm bringing it to You right
now and whenever it makes me fearful. Amen.

Fear Whom?

*The Lord is my light and the One Who saves me.
Whom should I fear? The Lord is the strength
of my life. Of whom should I be afraid?*

PSALM 27:1 NLV

People often hurt other people. It's easy to be anxious if we start imagining what harm could come to us whether from hackers or terrorists or just a backbiting "friend." We don't live in Mayberry anymore; maybe we never did.

How can we stay peaceful living in a world of evil? We must cling to the One who will be there for us no matter what others do to us. God is the light when all seems dark. He is salvation when all seems lost. He is our strength when it seems impossible to stand, let alone take another step. He is God with us, so whom should we fear?

*Lord, I get anxious when I think about the evil
things people do. May my heart say instead, "I
fear no one"—because You are my God. Amen.*

Our Intercessor

The Spirit helps us in our weakness. . . . The Spirit himself intercedes for us with groanings too deep for words. And he who searches hearts knows what is the mind of the Spirit, because the Spirit intercedes for the saints according to the will of God.

ROMANS 8:26–27 ESV

Have you ever been so anxious that you couldn't settle your heart to pray? Maybe you didn't know what to pray for or how to put it into words. Don't worry. When praying is hard, the Holy Spirit prays on our behalf.

God sees to the heart of us. No one—not even yourself—knows you better than the One who created every last cell in your body and has written every last day in His book (see Psalm 139). And His Spirit intercedes with soul-felt prayers, prayers that perfectly align your need with God's will.

Lord, I'm anxious. Let me sit awhile with You in silence while Your Holy Spirit prays for me. Amen.

Peace with God

Therefore, there is now no condemnation
for those who are in Christ Jesus.
ROMANS 8:1 NIV

It's one thing to be told you're forgiven. It's another thing to believe you're forgiven.

Once you trust in Jesus to save you, you are saved. Hallelujah! But at some point, the wily devil whispers in your ear, reminding you of your past sins, jeering over your present failures. Unease sets in, and you might think, *Am I really forgiven?*

God knows all about our sins. Yet out of His immense love, He offers to wipe the slate clean. He opens His arms and welcomes us back. And "since we have been justified through faith, *we have peace with God* through our Lord Jesus Christ" (Romans 5:1 NIV, italics added). No more condemnation. No more guilt. No more unease. Just fresh starts and full peace. What a wonderful God!

Lord, when I confess my sins, You promise to
forgive (1 John 1:9). I am so grateful! Thank
You for the peace I have in You. Amen.

God Pleasers

*Am I now trying to win the approval of human
beings, or of God? . . . If I were still trying to please
people, I would not be a servant of Christ.*

GALATIANS 1:10 NIV

No matter how self-confident we are, no matter how firm in our opinions, we care what people think about us, don't we? We become anxious, wondering if we're liked. We worry whether we're pleasing people.

The Bible frees us from those feelings. Yes, we should seek the other person's good. Yes, we should be considerate. But the one we ultimately look to for approval is God.

Jesus was the perfect person, and He was hated by many in His day. As we follow in His footsteps, we will be hated too. But we are blessed even then (Luke 6:22–23), which means we can be at peace even then.

---

*Lord, I worry I will look bad to other people.
I needed this reminder that when I live for
You, You look on me with approval. Amen.*

Sound Sleep

*Then [Jesus] got into the boat and his disciples
followed him. Suddenly a furious storm came
up on the lake, so that the waves swept
over the boat. But Jesus was sleeping.*

MATTHEW 8:23–24 NIV

Picture it: A tiny boat. A big lake. All is calm. All is fine. Then the wind picks up. The waves rise up. That tiny boat is now swamped by the big lake.

The disciples found themselves in just such a scene. Fearing the worst, they rushed to Jesus, and lo and behold, He was sound asleep. When your mind is calm, that same sound sleep may come easy. But when worries toss your thoughts around like a dinghy on a stormy sea? Sleep may not come at all.

What was Jesus' secret to sleeping through anything? Faith. Faith in the One who controls the wind and waves—the One right there in the boat with us.

---

*Lord, anxiety is keeping me awake many nights.
Increase my faith in You so that my sleep is sound. Amen.*

No Comparison

*I am sure that our suffering now cannot be compared
to the shining-greatness that He is going to give us.*
ROMANS 8:18 NLV

Ever worry about something for a while—then when that
something actually happens, it's not as bad as you worried it
would be? In fact, you wonder why you were worried at all.

Anxiety is like that. It can take legitimately daunting
things and enlarge them. It can also take small things and
make them seem ginormous. But as we filter our lives—along
with our anxiety—through God's lens, we gain a right perspective. The struggles of earth are as nothing compared to
the glory of heaven. So too our worries today fade when we
realize that God will get us to tomorrow.

And just think—if we look back now and wonder why
we were so worried, how insignificant will our worries look
when viewed from our glorious home!

Lord, help me see my worries as You see them. Amen.

Which Way?

In all your ways acknowledge him,
and he will make straight your paths.

PROVERBS 3:6 ESV

Every day we make decisions—what to wear, what to eat, what to buy, what to read. . . . Most of the time, our decisions don't cause anxiety. But what about those "turn this way or turn that way" choices—the choices that will change the course of our lives? Then the internal debates begin. Then our hearts anxiously ask, *What if I choose wrong?*

When we're anxious, God's Word has assurance that we are never alone to make decisions. Isaiah told God's people, "Whether you turn to the right or to the left, your ears will hear a voice behind you, saying, 'This is the way; walk in it'" (Isaiah 30:21 NIV). If we actively include God in everything we do, He helps us choose which way to turn. Indeed, He goes before us to make the paths straight.

Lord, whisper to my heart which way to go. Amen.

Nothing

*Who can keep us away from the love
of Christ? Can trouble or problems?
Can suffering wrong. . . ? Can it be
because of. . .danger or war?*
ROMANS 8:35 NLV

Paul, the author of Romans, posed an important question:
What can separate us from God's love? When Paul gave
the answer, he wasn't just hoping he was correct; he wasn't
almost-but-not-quite certain either. He was 100 percent
convinced. "I know that nothing can keep us from the love
of God. Death cannot! Life cannot! Angels cannot! Leaders
cannot! Any other power cannot! Hard things now or in the
future cannot! The world above or the world below cannot!
Any other living thing cannot keep us away from the love of
God" (Romans 8:38–39 NLV).

No matter how grim our circumstances, there remains a
bright spot on the horizon: God's love is here with us!

*Lord, soothe my anxieties with Your love—
love that not a thing can keep from me! Amen.*

In Your Midst

*"Fear not, O Zion. . . . The LORD your God is
in your midst. . .he will rejoice over you with
gladness; he will quiet you by his love."*
ZEPHANIAH 3:16–17 ESV

Biblical Israel's past was not placid. Their history is dotted with disobedience, slavery, captivity, and suffering. But despite all they went through—whether just desserts or undeserved—God was as faithful as ever. He *still* stands among His people, promising a brighter future, promising peace.

And that goes for everyone who calls Him their God. Despite all that has happened in our past, despite all that we're going through currently, God is in our midst. And His desire isn't simply to *be* there. He wants to bring gladness into our lives. He wants to soothe us. What an offer for those of us with anxious hearts! Why not take Him up on that?

---

*Lord, I'm letting go of all my anxiety
and letting You quiet my heart. Amen.*

Father God

*As a father has compassion on his children, so the LORD
has compassion on those who fear him; for he knows
how we are formed, he remembers that we are dust.*
PSALM 103:13–14 NIV

Way back in the beginning, God created a man from the
ground. He breathed life into the earthen frame, and He's
been breathing life into humankind ever since.

God, more than anyone else, knows our makeup. He
hasn't forgotten that we are but dust without Him. So it's
a good thing our Creator is also our Father, our Abba—our
Dad. He sees our anxieties. He sees our weaknesses. And
He—like the best of fathers—has compassion on us. We don't
have to put on a brave face around a God like that. We can
lay ourselves and our worries before Him and expect His
gentle hand to lift our chins and ease our burdens.

---

*Lord, all my worries are reminding me how
vulnerable I am. I'm coming to You now,
knowing You'll understand. Amen.*

Waiting

Wait for the Lord. Be strong. Let your heart be strong. Yes, wait for the Lord.

PSALM 27:14 NLV

Patience is a virtue. Though you won't find that saying in the Bible, the Bible does have something to say about patience. Believers are encouraged to be patient—even with God.

We certainly need the encouragement because one of the most difficult parts of the Christian life is waiting for God—waiting for Him to act on our behalf, waiting for Him to answer our prayers. What happens, for instance, when we make our requests to God and then He's silent? We may be restless until He responds. But we don't have to be. God says, "Those who hope in me will not be disappointed" (Isaiah 49:23 NIV). Whatever we're waiting on, once we surrender the outcome to God, there's no doubt that He will not let us down.

Lord, my heart isn't strong right now as I wait for You— it's anxious. Help me be patient for Your best. Amen.

Words to Live By

*Yes, even if I walk through the valley of
the shadow of death, I will not be afraid
of anything, because You are with me.*
PSALM 23:4 NLV

There's a reason why certain scripture passages have become favorites. Psalm 23 is one of them. The words pack a powerful punch of reassurance whenever we're anxious. Try repeating God's truth to yourself today: "The LORD is my shepherd, I lack nothing. He makes me lie down in green pastures, he leads me beside quiet waters, he refreshes my soul. He guides me along the right paths for his name's sake. Even though I walk through the darkest valley, I will fear no evil, for you are with me; your rod and your staff, they comfort me. . . . Surely your goodness and love will follow me all the days of my life" (Psalm 23:1–4, 6 NIV).

*Lord, thank You for Your Word, which is full of reminders
of Your protection, Your provision. . .Your presence. Amen.*

No Worrying

Do not worry. Learn to pray about everything. Give thanks to God as you ask Him for what you need.
PHILIPPIANS 4:6 NLV

If you're a worrywart, you know what it's like to worry about every single thing. What other people wouldn't give a second's thought to, you can fret over for hours. God's way of living is the reverse: "Do not be anxious about anything" (Philippians 4:6 NIV). *Anything*—as in nothing, nada, zilch. *How?* you ask. By praying about everything. Worrying won't take us out at the knees if we fall to our knees first and talk to God. Doing this consistently might not happen overnight, but remember, we weren't born worrying about everything. We've had lots of practice and learned to worry like that, which means we can learn to pray instead.

And what a wonderful day it will be when we realize that our prayers outnumber our worries.

---

*Lord, praying and not worrying is new
to me. Help me stick with it. Amen.*

Don't Lose Your Focus

Peter got out of the boat and walked on the water
to Jesus. But when he saw the strong wind, he
was afraid. He began to go down in the water.
MATTHEW 14:29–30 NLV

The disciples were cruising in a boat, and Jesus, wanting to join them, walked right across the sea. Undeterred by the freakish sight, Peter asked to walk on water too. Which he did. Until he laid eyes on the wind. Notably, the wind didn't suddenly start blowing once Peter's feet hit the water. It had already been windy before he exited the boat. The difference between walking and sinking wasn't what was going on—but what Peter was focusing on.

How like our lives! We may start out focused, but distractions and stress push in. What then? We'd best keep our eyes on Jesus, our faith centered on Him.

Lord, not being anxious isn't dependent on
my circumstances. Help me to not doubt
You but rather to depend on You. Amen.

Fearless Spirits

For God hath not given us the spirit of fear;
but of power, and of love, and of a sound mind.
2 TIMOTHY 1:7 KJV

Lots of things *could* intimidate us, but thanks to God, we don't have to *be* intimidated.

The Bible describes a God-given spirit of power and a sound mind, not fear. What may be most difficult for us to grasp—especially if we're used to feeling anxious—is that this fearless spirit isn't something yet to come; it already exists. Look at the verb in 2 Timothy 1:7 (NLV): "[God] gave us a spirit of power and of love and of a good mind." He *gave* us. A done deal. Signed and delivered. This spirit is already ours! It may be shoved dusty and forgotten behind years of worry, but the One who gave it will show us how to find it.

Lord, help me live in the spirit You've
given—strong and steady. Amen.

Material Worries

"Why do you worry about clothes? See how the flowers of the field grow. . . . Not even Solomon in all his splendor was dressed like one of these. If that is how God clothes the grass of the field. . .will he not much more clothe you?"

MATTHEW 6:28–30 NIV

We shop for stuff. We snag bargains on stuff. We look for more stuff. We worry we don't have the newest stuff or enough stuff. . . . Maybe that's you, maybe not, but lots of women exhaust considerable time and energy on material possessions. And Jesus asks, "Why?"

Why do we allow *things* to cause us anxiety? In themselves, our possessions aren't the problem. Having stuff isn't wrong. But when our possessions own us, we must stop and remember that God bought us with Jesus' blood and won't neglect our needs now—or ever.

Let's look past our stuff to our Savior.

Lord, stuff is distracting and worrying me. I'm choosing to spend myself on You instead. Amen.

Oh, Work!

You rise up early, and go to bed late, and work hard for your food, all for nothing. For the Lord gives to His loved ones even while they sleep.

PSALM 127:2 NLV

Getting up early. Going to bed late. Working hard. . .and it's all for nothing? Should we ditch our work ethic and sleep in, then? No. The Bible doesn't support an all-play-and-no-work lifestyle. The sluggard is told to learn from the hardworking ant (Proverbs 6:6–11), and Paul bluntly stated that the one who won't work won't eat (2 Thessalonians 3:10).

But if we're stressing ourselves out with overwork so we feel good about ourselves and our future, we've got it wrong. We're working for ourselves, not for God, when we could give our work our best and then relax. God will provide—yes, even while we're doing nothing but sleeping.

Lord, where is my hard work necessary and pleasing to You, and where am I creating stress for myself? Amen.

Chasing after God

I have seen all the things that are done under the sun;
all of them are meaningless, a chasing after the wind.
ECCLESIASTES 1:14 NIV

Reading Ecclesiastes can be a bit of a downer. The word *meaningless* is used four times in the second verse alone: "'Meaningless! Meaningless!' says the Teacher. 'Utterly meaningless! Everything is meaningless'" (Ecclesiastes 1:2 NIV).

But haven't we felt that way ourselves? We work, we play, and we're no better off. We run in circles, brimming with anxiety, yet we always end up right back where we started. . . like we're chasing after the wind.

So what can we conclude? Life is meaningless? Well, that depends on where you find meaning. If this life itself is the be-all and end-all, then yes. But if this life is about living for God, it has meaning now and eternally.

Lord, when life feels pointless, point me to
You. I don't want to chase what's unfulfilling.
I want to chase after You! Amen.

Like a Weaned Child

I have calmed and quieted my soul,
like a weaned child with its mother;
like a weaned child is my soul within me.
PSALM 131:2 ESV

There's nothing quite like anxiety to put us out of sorts. Anxiety can muddle our thinking, twist our stomachs, shorten our fuse, and fray our nerves. In short, we're uncomfortable and discontented—like colicky babes who need soothing. . . and not much like the child that David compared himself to in Psalm 131:2 (NIV): "I have calmed and quieted myself, I am like a weaned child with its mother; like a weaned child I am content." Just as a child who has learned to trust her mother can sit calmly and quietly in her mother's lap, David could settle himself in God's presence. David was a child without a care because God, his Father, was near. And God is near us too.

Lord, teach me how to stop fussing, how to let my heart be still, because You're looking after me! Amen.

Rivers in His Hand

The heart of the king is like rivers of water in the
hand of the Lord. He turns it where He wishes.
PROVERBS 21:1 NLV

Corrupt leaders aren't a modern phenomenon. History books record the wickedness of rulers going back thousands of years. And no matter when it happens—whether in ancient times or the twenty-first century—bad leadership causes fear. We worry where our nation is headed. We panic as we watch events spin out of control.

Yet the truth is nothing is out of God's control—even politics. Not one leader comes to power without God's say-so (Romans 13:1). What's more, not one leader is beyond God's power to direct as He chooses. So when seeking peace, the question we must ask ourselves isn't if we can trust our leaders—but if we can trust the King who reigns over all kings.

Lord, I don't understand why You allow evil
to lead, but I believe You are making a way for
good. Reassure me of Your power today. Amen.

Be Still And. . .

He says, "Be still, and know that I am God."
PSALM 46:10 NIV

When something is wrong, how many of us are content to fold our hands and let God take over? When we're worried, don't we want to *do* something—anything—to ease the tension? Our natural inclination isn't to sit still.

So God doesn't just tell us to be still. He pairs one command with another that tells us why to be still. "Be still, and know that I am God." He might as easily have said, "Be still, because I am God." God is God, and that means we can "let be and be still" (Psalm 46:10 AMPC). He has everything well in hand.

The next time anxiety makes you restless, try being still—in body and in mind. Try taking a moment to reflect on who God is.

Lord, I am restless. Help me be still.
Help me know that You are God. Amen.

Constant God

Whatever is good and perfect comes to us from God. He is the One Who made all light. He does not change. No shadow is made by His turning.

JAMES 1:17 NLV

Some days, it seems all you have to do is blink and things change. Our world isn't static, that's for sure. And sooner or later, the shifts affect our lives personally. Despite the unpredictability of life, though, we don't have to dread what we'll wake up to each morning. Through every change, God remains unchanged. Our Lord is the same yesterday, today, and for infinite tomorrows (Hebrews 13:8). We can count on Him to be there and to be full of goodness and light.

Focus on the world, and it will leave you dizzy with its turning. But focus on the One who doesn't turn—and your world is suddenly steady.

Lord, help me worry less about what will change and think more about You, who doesn't ever change. Amen.

Future Plans

*"For I am God, and there is no other. I am
God, and there is no one like Me. I tell from the
beginning what will happen in the end. And from
times long ago I tell of things which have not
been done, saying, 'My Word will stand.'"*

ISAIAH 46:9–10 NLV

Horoscopes, palm readers, fortune cookies, soothsayers. . .
Humans have been trying to predict the future forever, but
even in Bible times the attempt was vain if not disastrous.
God told the people, "Call the star watchers, those who tell
by the stars what will happen in the future. . . . Have them
stand up and save you from what will come upon you. See,
they have become like dry grass" (Isaiah 47:13–14 NLV).

The future isn't ours to know. But it is God's. And He
not only sees time spread out before Him—He plans what
will happen.

*Lord, I can't see ahead, but I'm choosing to
trust You for the future, come what may. Amen.*

Take to Heart

*"I have treasured the words of his
mouth more than my daily bread."*

JOB 23:12 NIV

Memorizing scripture is a popular theme among Christians today, but learning God's Word by heart got its start long ago. Moses, speaking about God's Law to the people, urged them, "Fix these words of mine in your hearts and minds" (Deuteronomy 11:18 NIV). And the psalmist wrote, "I have hidden your word in my heart" (Psalm 119:11 NIV).

When scripture was written on giant scrolls, memorizing it was a necessity, but why is it such a big deal now that the Bible can fit in a pocket?

God's Word is alive (Hebrews 4:12); when we make it part of us, it supports our lives (Matthew 4:4). And when we need to calm ourselves—deep breath in, deep breath out—God-breathed scripture (2 Timothy 3:16) is like God's breath in our hearts.

---

*Lord, what verses should I keep in my
heart to keep anxiety away? Amen.*

Until Troubles Pass

*Be merciful unto me, O God, be merciful unto me: for my
soul trusteth in thee: yea, in the shadow of thy wings will
I make my refuge, until these calamities be overpast.*

PSALM 57:1 KJV

Sometimes we're met with such staggering trouble we can't
help but be overwhelmed. We can't stop our hearts from
worrying any more than we could've stopped the troubles
themselves. What's a girl to do then? Pray.

Go straight to God. Remember, God is our refuge, our
strength; He is "a *very present* help in trouble" (Psalm 46:1
ESV, italics added). God isn't some far-off deity who observes
our troubles. He is near, welcoming us to seek respite in His
presence. The psalmist said it well: "My soul goes to You to
be safe. And I will be safe in the shadow of Your wings until
the trouble has passed" (Psalm 57:1 NLV).

---

*Lord, I'm seeking You in my troubles. Wrap
Your wings around me. Hide me in Your
presence until this trouble passes. Amen.*

Fret Not

Do not trouble yourself because of sinful men. . . .
For they will soon dry up like the grass. Like the green
plant they will soon die. Trust in the Lord, and do good.
PSALM 37:1–3 NLV

The guilty person gets off scot-free. The bully gets away with bullying. The unscrupulous get rich. . . . You can probably think of many more examples of bad people who seem to get by just fine in this life while the innocent suffer. We could spend time fretting and fuming about it, but the Bible says, "Fret not thyself because of evildoers" (Psalm 37:1 KJV).

Why shouldn't we bother worrying about these people? For one thing, God will deal with evil and evildoers. And for another, time used up fretting cannot be used again. Let's choose to use our time on what's good.

Lord, I do let sinful people trouble me. Help
me trust You and do good instead. Amen.

Watch Out

Keep awake! Watch at all times. The devil is working against you. He is walking around like a hungry lion with his mouth open. He is looking for someone to eat.

1 PETER 5:8 NLV

This probably won't surprise you, but the devil wants us to fail. He is not for us but against us. Nothing would make him happier than us giving up. So the Bible pictures him as a predator stalking its prey.

The devil's vendetta holds true for our anxiety. Say we set our hearts to trust and not worry. Then—wouldn't you know?—new reasons to worry surface out of nowhere. Our enemy reaches into his arsenal of doubts and lobs one at us.

Thankfully, we've been warned and aren't unarmed. Don't allow the devil to catch you unawares. Be watchful. Be prayerful. Fight enemy fire with faith.

Lord, the devil may be working against me, but You are here, helping me withstand. That alone gives peace to my anxious heart. Amen.

Through the Trials

*"When you pass through the waters, I will be with you.
When you pass through the rivers, they will not flow
over you. When you walk through the fire, you will not
be burned. The fire will not destroy you. For I am the
Lord your God, the Holy One of Israel, Who saves you."*

ISAIAH 43:2–3 NLV

The Bible never gives false hope about trials—that we can somehow escape every one. God doesn't say "if" you go through hard times; He says "when." Surely no one can reach the end of life without passing through the flood and the fire sometime.

But for us who believe in Jesus, we are given true hope—that our God will be with us in the trials, that He will bring us through the trials. Oh, hard times will happen, but God is our shield, our strength, and our Savior in each one.

---

*Lord, some trials I can't imagine living through.
I won't worry though. I will hope in You. Amen.*

Spiritual Training

Growing strong in body is all right but growing in God-like living is more important. It will not only help you in this life now but in the next life also.

1 TIMOTHY 4:8 NLV

You can find lots of tips online for dealing with anxiety. Many focus on physical remedies like exercise and deep breathing. While those things are helpful, they are not the most important.

In his letter to Timothy, Paul wrote that bodily training is useful, but spiritual training is more so. His reasoning is simple: because life on earth is temporary and life in heaven is eternal, spiritual training is a long-term investment that will serve us well now *and* forever.

If we really want to reduce anxiety, we must go deeper than our bodies. We must treat our souls. Scripture, praise, prayer—these grow us in ways that make for peace now as well as make us ready for Paradise.

Lord, help me to not neglect spiritual things as I deal with my anxiety. Amen.

Anxiety Conquered

*Who shall separate us from the love of Christ? shall
tribulation, or distress, or persecution, or famine, or
nakedness, or peril, or sword? . . . Nay, in all these things
we are more than conquerors through him that loved us.*

ROMANS 8:35, 37 KJV

Because God loved us, we are spared hell itself. And through
this God of love, we are made conquerors over the unconquerable. We are *more than* conquerors, in fact, over tribulation,
distress, persecution, famine, nakedness, peril, sword. "We
have power over all these things through Jesus Who loves
us so much" (Romans 8:37 NLV).

Anxiety may seem unconquerable. But considering everything else God makes us conquerors over, you can bet
anxiety isn't above Him. The point we mustn't miss is that
we are conquerors *through* Him. Through Him we will more
than conquer anxiety.

---

*Lord, I've tried to conquer anxiety on my own but not
anymore. Thank You for Your love and the promise of
being more than a conqueror through You. Amen.*

Dependable Peace

"God is not human, that he should lie, not a human being, that he should change his mind. Does he speak and then not act? Does he promise and not fulfill?"
NUMBERS 23:19 NIV

People have likely disappointed you a time or two. . .or more. We humans overcommit and make promises we don't keep. God isn't like that—not in the least. After a lifetime of following God, Joshua told God's people, "You know with all your heart and soul that not one of all the good promises the LORD your God gave you has failed. Every promise has been fulfilled; not one has failed" (Joshua 23:14 NIV). When God gives His word, He means it. He won't fall short of His promises. So when He says He gives peace unlike the world's, which is sketchy at best (see John 14:27), we can depend on exactly that.

---

*Lord, I need peace. You promise peace.
May I not doubt that You will deliver. Amen.*

In Perspective

*All that is in the world—the desires of the flesh
and the desires of the eyes and pride of life—is
not from the Father but is from the world. And the
world is passing away along with its desires, but
whoever does the will of God abides forever.*

1 JOHN 2:16–17 ESV

Do you get hung up on little things? Things like "Was my text message dumb?" or "Should I have picked a different paint color?" Even to a worrier, some worries sound trivial. Trouble is, we can't always recognize when we're stuck in trivial worries.

Whenever we worry, it helps to widen our focus. As Christians, we aren't to cling to this life; we're reaching for the next. Although this world is our home for now, it's passing away, and when it goes, everything in it goes too.

Why worry about something that won't matter in eternity?

Lord, change my perspective so I don't worry about trivial things. What matters is doing Your will. Amen.

Think about This

*Keep your minds thinking about whatever is true,
whatever is respected, whatever is right, whatever
is pure, whatever can be loved, and whatever is
well thought of. If there is anything good and worth
giving thanks for, think about these things.*

PHILIPPIANS 4:8 NLV

Random thoughts may pop into our minds, but what we choose to think about is indeed a choice. In Philippians 4:8, the Bible lists what our minds should dwell on. If a thought isn't true, respected, right, pure, etc., then we shouldn't give it a second thought. Our anxious thoughts don't meet the criteria, so we need to think other thoughts. And yes, that takes effort. We don't just let our minds think about good things; we *keep* our minds thinking about them. That may seem like an impossible task at first. Never mind. Just take it one thought at a time.

*Lord, I'll need help thinking differently. I want
to think about the things Your Word says
to think about, not my worries. Amen.*

Feeling Pressured?

*He has shown you, O mortal, what is good. And what
does the LORD require of you? To act justly and to
love mercy and to walk humbly with your God.*

MICAH 6:8 NIV

We women have a lot on our plate just with work, family,
and church. But then we scoop on more. We add community
projects, fitness regimens, social media, PTA, clubs. We put
pressure on ourselves to do it all. Sometimes that pressure
seeps into our spiritual lives too. God must want *more* from
us, mustn't He?

The prophet Micah addressed that issue. He asked,
"What does the LORD require of you?" We might expect a
long list of shalls and shall-nots, but what we get is short and
sweet: "To act justly and to love mercy and to walk humbly
with your God." Thousands of sacrifices won't please God
as much as simply living in step with Him (Micah 6:6–8).

*Lord, thank You for taking the pressure off.
May Your requirements be mine too. Amen.*

Until Completion

I am sure of this, that he who began a good work in you
will bring it to completion at the day of Jesus Christ.
PHILIPPIANS 1:6 ESV

When learning to overcome anxiety, it may feel like a one step forward, two steps back process at times. You may wonder if you're making any progress at all. Don't be discouraged. God isn't.

From the moment you believed in Jesus, God has been transforming you. He's been replacing old habits with new. He's been rewriting your character. He's been reworking you into the image of His Son. You may not see progress, but God hasn't stopped. "God Who began the good work in you will keep on working in you" (Philippians 1:6 NLV). So keep on trusting God through every struggle and apparent setback. Trust that He always finishes what He's started.

Lord, I'm frustrated by how anxious I still get.
But that doesn't mean You aren't doing something
in me. Help me see the progress You're making. Amen.

Rest

*"Come to me, all you who are weary and burdened,
and I will give you rest. Take my yoke upon you
and learn from me, for I am gentle and humble
in heart, and you will find rest for your souls.
For my yoke is easy and my burden is light."*
MATTHEW 11:28–30 NIV

A long day of worrying will leave us mentally exhausted and even physically drained. We crave rest. We want to stop the mind's wheels from turning and slough off the worries.

Jesus offers the rest we crave. He offers ultimate rest for our souls—salvation. He also offers daily rest for our hearts. Jesus' way of living isn't the anxious rat race we're used to; it's a steady walk alongside our Savior. Jesus doesn't load us with burdens; He takes our burdens from us (Psalm 55:22; Isaiah 53:4).

"Come to Me," He's saying. "Learn from Me." And we will rest.

Oh, to rest, Lord! Let me find my rest in You. Amen.

The Valleys

Though I walk through the valley of the shadow
of death, I will fear no evil. . .thou art with me.

PSALM 23:4 KJV

How we respond to serious—perhaps even life-or-death—problems says heaps about our faith. Or, more accurately, it reveals where we're putting our faith.

David was familiar with danger. Even before he battled Israel's enemies, his job as a shepherd meant facing down lions and bears. Later, when David faced down a giant, he gave a reason for his courage: "The LORD who rescued me from the paw of the lion and the paw of the bear will rescue me from the hand of this Philistine.. . ."I come against you in the name of the LORD Almighty" (1 Samuel 17:37, 45 NIV).

We'll fall apart if our faith is in ourselves. But with faith in God, we can face the worst with courage and with peace.

Lord, though I walk through valleys,
I have faith that You are with me. Amen.

Held Tight

*"I know them, and they follow me.... No one
will snatch them out of my hand. My Father, who
has given them to me, is greater than all; no one
can snatch them out of my Father's hand."*

JOHN 10:27–29 NIV

In troubled times, it's a good idea to hold tight to God. The worst thing we can do when we're overwhelmed is throw up our hands and let the troubles keep us from Him.

Easily said, we may think. *Not always so easily done.* What if our harried days result in neglected Bibles? What if sheer weariness causes us to fall asleep midprayer? . . . We are still held tight. Even when our grip loosens, God's grip doesn't. He holds our lives as firmly as ever, and nothing will change that.

Lord, I'm afraid I'm not staying as close to You as I should. Thank You for the security of You holding me tight. Amen.

Abiding

"Abide in me, and I in you."

If your desire is to grow in faith, you look forward to seeing good fruit in your life. But before any of us expects to bear fruit, we need a lesson in spiritual horticulture. Here's what Jesus taught: "As the branch cannot bear fruit by itself, unless it abides in the vine, neither can you, unless you abide in me. I am the vine; you are the branches. Whoever abides in me and I in him, he it is that bears much fruit, for apart from me you can do nothing" (John 15:4–5 ESV).

How much of our lack of peace and abundance of anxiety stems from the fact that we don't abide in Jesus? We're like orchids living in the hollow of a tree rather than branches drawing life from the vine. But when we abide in Jesus 24-7, He sees to it that we see much fruit.

Lord, teach me more about abiding in You. Amen.

Ask Nature

"But ask the animals, and they will teach you, or the birds in the sky, and they will tell you; or speak to the earth, and it will teach you, or let the fish in the sea inform you. . . . In [God's] hand is the life of every creature and the breath of all mankind."

JOB 12:7–8, 10 NIV

We live in a high-tech society with nature on the outskirts. Some of us might go an entire day without stepping foot outside. That's a far cry from our first ancestors. God made Adam and Eve and placed them in a garden.

While it's maybe not practical to pull up stakes and relocate to a garden, nature still has a lot to give us. Just being outdoors can be healing. And beyond that healing quality, nature tells us about God. We see who He is and how He cares for all creation, including us.

---

*Lord, show me ways I can discover peace—
and You—through nature. Amen.*

To Boast or Not to Boast

Not that we dare to classify or compare
ourselves with some of those who are
commending themselves. But when they
measure themselves by one another and
compare themselves with one another,
they are without understanding.

2 CORINTHIANS 10:12 ESV

Boasting seems commonplace nowadays. Social media gives us a platform to share the happenings in our lives, but aren't a lot of those posts actually boasts?

Paul wrote about boasting. He wasn't an antiboaster necessarily—he boasted in weaknesses (2 Corinthians 12:9) and he boasted in the Lord (1 Corinthians 1:31; Galatians 6:14). But he also warned against prideful speaking and the pitfall of comparing ourselves with others.

Trying to measure up—especially if you don't think you have anything to boast about—can cause anxiety. What if instead we looked to God for our worth? What if we let Him give us reasons to boast (see 2 Corinthians 10:13)?

Lord, help me have understanding when it
comes to boasting. Please keep my heart
from comparing and worrying. Amen.

Priceless Beauty

Your beauty should come from the inside. It should come from the heart. This is the kind that lasts. Your beauty should be a gentle and quiet spirit. In God's sight this is of great worth.

1 PETER 3:4 NLV

Even though what people think of as beautiful varies, when they say a woman is beautiful, they typically mean her face or figure—her appearance—is beautiful. God looks inside first (1 Samuel 16:7). Yes, God admires *inner beauty*. So should we; yet from the time we're teenagers, or younger, we begin to worry about our outer beauty. We may take great pains to be beautiful outwardly. Isn't it time we focused inwardly?

God will make over our spirits as we spend time with Him. We'll become ever more beautiful in His sight. . .and He will slowly change our thinking so we see that beauty too.

Lord, I'm beautiful to You. Help me not worry about my appearance but care about my spirit. Amen.

A Time for Everything

*There is a time for everything, and a season
for every activity under the heavens. . . . [God]
has made everything beautiful in its time.*
ECCLESIASTES 3:1, 11 NIV

Are you a "live in the moment" type of person? Or are you always wishing for what's next? If we want something to happen—say, to get married or to have a baby or to find a job or to heal from an illness—we also want it to happen quickly. Problem is, we miss life now by anxiously awaiting the next season.

The Bible tells us that there is a time for everything, and it's not a matter of stars finally aligning or chance. The King James Version translates Ecclesiastes 3:11 as "he hath made every thing beautiful in *his* time" (italics added). There is a time for everything—but all in good time. All in God's timing.

Lord, You know how anxious I am for certain things to happen. Please give me faith to trust Your timing. Amen.

Faithful Prayers

*Rejoice in hope, be patient in
tribulation, be constant in prayer.*
ROMANS 12:12 ESV

The tornado siren blares. The family hunkers down in the basement. As the wind beats against the house, someone says, "All we can do now is pray." Those words have been said in hospital waiting rooms, in disaster areas, in war zones, in the hours before the phone rings. . . . But why is prayer sometimes the last thing we do? Considering what the Bible says about believers' prayers—"The eyes of the LORD are toward the righteous and his ears toward their cry. . . . When the righteous cry for help, the LORD hears and delivers them out of all their troubles" (Psalm 34:15, 17 ESV)—prayer should be our first resort.

"Be constant in prayer"—wise words indeed, because when our prayers are as steady as our heartbeat in normal times, they will steady our hearts in dire times too.

Lord, may I be as faithful to pray as You are to hear. Amen.

Put to the Test

*"In the desert He fed you bread from heaven,
which your fathers did not know about. He did
this so you would not have pride and that He
might test you. It was for your good in the end."*

DEUTERONOMY 8:16 NLV

God parted the Red Sea. Really think about that. Israel was trapped between an army and a sea, and God made a way *through the water*. Clearly God could take care of His people. Yet not quite three months later, His people were worried that they would starve. God provided again—this time manna and quail. But eventually Israel doubted again; they even doubted God's promise of the Promised Land. The entire generation who had seen God part a sea and rain food from heaven missed out on a huge blessing.

Our wildernesses are testing grounds. Don't test God though. Let Him test you. And let Him bless you in the end.

---

*Lord, help me trust and obey
You in every situation. Amen.*

Peace in God

Every man walks here and there like a shadow.
He makes a noise about nothing. He stores up
riches, not knowing who will gather them. And
now, Lord, what do I wait for? My hope is in You.
PSALM 39:6–7 NLV

Sometimes only a few minutes in the world are enough to make your head spin. Everybody rushing from one place to another. Everybody grabbing for their slice of the pie before it's gone. Everybody shouting to be heard. Not exactly the atmosphere for peace, is it?

No, peace isn't in this world of noise and bustle and strain. Everybody is after something. We may call it different names—success, security, pleasure. . . . But what we're really after—deep down, at soul level—is God. Peace only comes from pinning our hopes on Him.

Lord, it's all too easy to get caught up
in the world, and then my peace is gone.
Help me center myself in You again. Amen.

Praise God!

*Praise the LORD. Praise God in his sanctuary;
praise him in his mighty heavens. Praise
him for his acts of power; praise him for his
surpassing greatness. . . . Let everything that
has breath praise the LORD. Praise the LORD.*
PSALM 150:1–2, 6 NIV

Psalm 150 uses the word *praise* thirteen times in six verses.
And why not? Our God is holy and awesome. He is worthy
of every last breath of praise we give Him—and then some!

Want to put worries out of your mind? Fill your mind
with praises. Worrying and praising at the same time is a
little like an uncoordinated person trying to rub their belly
and pat their head at the same time. They'll probably end
up rubbing or patting both belly and head. Once we start
praising, our worrying might morph into a "rub-pat" at first. . .
until it becomes nothing but praise.

---

*Lord, why do I waste so much time worrying
when there's so much to praise You for? Amen.*

Worship God!

Come, let us bow down in worship, let
us kneel before the LORD our Maker.
PSALM 95:6 NIV

Worship goes hand in hand with praise. We may even think of them as one and the same. But worship is more than singing God's praises. Our *lives* are supposed to worship God. Paul wrote, "I urge you, brothers and sisters, in view of God's mercy, to offer your bodies as a living sacrifice, holy and pleasing to God—this is your true and proper worship" (Romans 12:1 NIV). It may seem strange to us if worshipping has always been reserved for worship services, but the way we live can be an act of worship.

What does this have to do with anxious hearts? Choosing to trust instead of worry honors God. In not allowing anxiety to rule, we're bowing to our King.

Lord, You are the One I worship. Help my life reflect
that. May I be a worshipper—not a worrier! Amen.

A Friend in High Places

Ascribe power to God, whose majesty is over Israel,
and whose power is in the skies. Awesome is God
from his sanctuary; the God of Israel—he is the one
who gives power and strength to his people.

PSALM 68:34–35 ESV

God isn't a deity who deigns to be among us—He *wants* to be among us! Think of Him fellowshipping with Adam and Eve in the Garden or of John lounging next to Jesus at the supper table (John 13:23). Even now, God is planning the day when He will dwell with us in heaven. It really is a blessing to call God our Friend.

But when we are anxious, we need to remember that He is God too. . .the God who spoke the world into existence, the God who speaks and His will is done. What an awesome God! So why be anxious when the Most High calls us His friends (see John 15:15)?

Lord, thank You that You are my
Friend and my God. Amen.

Rooted in the Storm

Have your roots planted deep in Christ.
Grow in Him. Get your strength from Him.
Let Him make you strong in the faith.
COLOSSIANS 2:7 NLV

A flimsy plant with shallow roots has good reason to fear the storm. A brisk breeze could blow it over! But a tree with roots gripping deep into solid ground? A tree like that can withstand storm after storm.

We tend to anticipate life's storms with dread, don't we? They're coming; we're sure of it. But we're not so sure how we'll fare. Paul faced storms as a Christian too—actual storms at sea and figurative storms of life. His advice? "Have your roots planted deep in Christ. . . . Get your strength from Him." Then the desert winds can batter and the storm blast, *yet we will withstand.*

I need deeper roots, Lord. Please help me grow in You.
Make my faith strong to endure any storm. Amen.

Good for the Heart

How happy he is whose wrong-doing
is forgiven, and whose sin is covered!
PSALM 32:1 NLV

God won't wink at sin in our lives. Why would He ignore what cost Him dearly to free us from? So His Spirit convicts our hearts. Sometimes He won't let us rest until we deal with our sin. Take it from King David—a guilty conscience equals inner turmoil, but confession is relief: "When I kept quiet about my sin, my bones wasted away from crying all day long. For day and night Your hand was heavy upon me. . . . I told my sin to You. I did not hide my wrong-doing. . . . And You forgave the guilt of my sin. So let all who are God-like pray to You while You may be found, because in the floods of much water, they will not touch him" (Psalm 32:3–6 NLV).

Lord, I've been hiding sin, but it's only tearing
me up inside. Here I am, confessing. . . . Amen.

Added Peace

*My son, do not forget my teaching. Let your
heart keep my words. For they will add to you
many days and years of life and peace.*
PROVERBS 3:1–2 NLV

Have you ever thought of the Bible as a manual—a how-to
book of sorts for life? From cover to cover, the Bible tells us
how to live: how to live eternally through faith in Jesus, and
how to live wisely on earth.

The value of wisdom may be lost on us, especially when
we're young. Living wisely doesn't sound very exciting, and
we'd rather do whatever we want. Solomon cautioned his son
about such a mindset because wisdom promises something
thrills cannot—"days and years of life and peace." Think
that's an exaggerated claim? Just consider how rotten it
feels to disregard wise advice and later worry about the
consequences. By following God's Word, we spare ourselves
a ton of anxious moments.

*Lord, I know firsthand the peace that comes with heeding
Your wisdom. May I keep Your words close. Amen.*

Trust in Him

*Trust in the LORD with all your heart and
lean not on your own understanding.*

PROVERBS 3:5 NIV

Imagine driving along the coast and stopping at a cliff overlooking the ocean. There's a fence at the edge, and you head over to take some pictures. Then you lean against the fence to soak up the view. Only, the metal post has rusted through, and it snaps under your weight. Uh-oh!

We like to think of our understanding as sturdy. We're logical and smart, and we've been around the block, so we know what to expect. But so often our understanding fails us. Life can't always be explained. It surprises us too—with surprises that might not be welcome. Thankfully, we have an alternative to leaning on our understanding: trusting in God Himself. He is the One to lean on wholeheartedly because He will never give out beneath us.

---

*Lord, I try to make sense of life, but I realize now
that I should be trusting You with life. Amen.*

Looking Forward

*I keep going on to make that life my own as
Christ Jesus made me His own. No, Christian
brothers, I do not have that life yet. But I do one
thing. I forget everything that is behind me and
look forward to that which is ahead of me.*

PHILIPPIANS 3:12–13 NLV

Anxiety usually centers on the future. We worry about what
could be. But we can also worry about the past—what could
have been. And fretting over our mistakes, our choices, or our
should'ves will stall us as effectively as fretting over what-ifs.

It seems Paul would have none of that. He'd have been the
first to admit he wasn't perfect, yet he wouldn't allow his past
to hold him back. He wouldn't allow water under the bridge
to keep him from crossing over the bridge! Let's not either.

---

*Lord, I'm worrying about things I cannot change.
Help me forget and look forward. Amen.*

To the Full

*"The thief comes only to steal and
kill and destroy; I have come that they
may have life, and have it to the full."*

JOHN 10:10 NIV

Good times tinged with worry, bad times made worse by worry—this was never the life God intended for us.

When Jesus came to earth, the life He had in mind was not some austere, fretful existence. "I have come that they may have life," He said, *"and have it to the full"* (John 10:10 NIV, italics added). "They will come in and go out, and find pasture" (John 10:9 NIV). To live fully, to live freely—that's the kind of living God intends. And it's a kind of living He makes possible through Jesus. There's no other way but the Way, no other life but the Life. All we have to do is enter.

---

*Lord, show me how to live to the
full this life I have in You! Amen.*

Believe!

"Why are you troubled, and why do doubts
arise in your hearts? See my hands
and my feet, that it is I myself."
LUKE 24:38–39 ESV

The news of Jesus' resurrection was spreading among His followers. Two of them were journeying to Emmaus—deep in conversation, unsure what to make of the news—when Jesus began walking beside them. After listening for a while, He exclaimed, "O foolish ones, and slow of heart to believe all that the prophets have spoken!" (Luke 24:25 ESV). Later that same day, the pair along with the Eleven were troubled when Jesus appeared. Jesus asked them why. And come to think of it, why were they troubled? Hadn't they heard a word God had said about His Son?

We could ask ourselves the same questions. God has spoken to us through His Word. His truths are laid out for us to see. And still we're troubled and doubtful. How about we believe Him instead?

Please bless me with belief, Lord. Amen.

Troubles Poured Out

Trust in him at all times. . .pour out your
hearts to him, for God is our refuge.
PSALM 62:8 NIV

Growing up, did you have a friend you could tell absolutely everything? Maybe your mom or a sister is the one you go to with your heartbreaks and worries. Confidants are true blessings when troubles fill our hearts. We shouldn't keep all our anxiety bottled up inside. . .but we shouldn't pour it out on just anyone either.

As Christians, we are blessed with the best confidant— one who will never betray us, one who will always be there for us. God. The psalmist wrote, "Trust in Him at all times, O people. Pour out your heart before Him. God is a safe place for us" (Psalm 62:8 NLV). God loves us greatly; He couldn't care more about us. And we're invited to share absolutely everything with Him!

Lord, thank You for hearing these
words from my heart. . . . Amen.

Stay Awhile

Whoever dwells in the shelter of the Most High
will rest in the shadow of the Almighty.
PSALM 91:1 NIV

Whether we're naturally restless or still, talkative or quiet, prayer takes practice. Let's face it, we can't see God and we can't audibly hear God, so praying can sometimes feel like talking into empty space. We might fill that space with our words, or we might rush through our prayers to get back to tangible things. But what would happen if we learned to settle down and just sit with God instead? What if we could quiet our anxious hearts and just be in His presence? What sweet rest would we find then? And what would God's Spirit communicate to our spirits in the silence? We'll never know until we try.

Lord, You're calling me to stay awhile. . .to just spend
time with You. I'm not very good at that—and I'm even
worse at it when I'm anxious. Help me as I try. Amen.

Weakness or Strength?

Most gladly therefore will I rather glory in my infirmities, that the power of Christ may rest upon me. . . . I take pleasure in infirmities, in reproaches, in necessities, in persecutions, in distresses for Christ's sake: for when I am weak, then am I strong.

2 CORINTHIANS 12:9–10 KJV

Something that makes us feel anxious makes us feel strong, right? Wrong. If anything, our anxieties highlight our weaknesses. But this isn't necessarily a negative. The Bible has lots of counterintuitive truths—truths like "the one who loses his life gains it" and "blessed are those who mourn." In Bible logic, our weaknesses can be our strength. The things that make us most anxious are chances to be our strongest. Why? Because the moment we realize how insufficient we are in ourselves is the moment we're able to realize how all-sufficient Christ is in us.

Lord, show Your strength where I am weak. Amen.

Self-Watch

*"Watch yourselves! . . . Do not be troubled with
the cares of this life. If you do, that day will
come on you without you knowing it."*

LUKE 21:34 NLV

Jesus told us that He is coming back. Our challenge isn't
to predict *when* but to stay alert until then. Particularly, we
are to monitor *ourselves*: "Be careful, or your hearts will be
weighed down with. . .the anxieties of life, and that day will
close on you suddenly like a trap" (Luke 21:34 NIV).

One way anxiety works against us is by causing us to lose
sight of spiritual matters. We're so busy with today's troubles
that we forget what day today may be. But if we treat every
day as if Jesus is due any minute? That would reshape how
we live—and how we worry.

---

*Lord, sometimes all I see is today and its worries.
I'm going to start watching myself more so my
heart will be watching for You! Amen.*

Need Wisdom?

If any of you lacks wisdom, you should ask God, who gives generously to all without finding fault, and it will be given to you.

JAMES 1:5 NIV

Has your brain ever felt like a ping-pong ball swatted back and forth when you had to make a decision? You think you've decided. Then *ping*—you think you should do something else. Then *pong*—you think maybe you should stick with that first decision. *Ping. Pong. Ping. Pong.* Now what?

Decisions need wisdom. When we're anxiously wondering what to do, we can ask God. He won't hold back His wisdom, and He won't hold our asking against us. But we do need to believe that we'll get what we ask for. Otherwise, we're "like a wave of the sea, blown and tossed by the wind" (James 1:6 NIV)—ping-ponging again.

Lord, I don't know what to decide, but I know I can count on You for wisdom. Guide me as I read the Bible and pray about this decision. Amen.

The Secret

*I know how to get along with little and how
to live when I have much. I have learned the
secret of being happy at all times. . . . I can do
all things because Christ gives me the strength.*
PHILIPPIANS 4:12–13 NLV

When we're up against hard times, it's easy to think we won't get through them. The bills may be stacking up, and the funds are dwindling. The deadline may be approaching, and we're running out of steam. Or the diagnosis is staggering, and our options are few.

Paul wrote of material needs in this passage from Philippians, but his message of content living applies just as well when we lack in nonmaterial ways too. The secret to getting through anything with peace and confidence—not anxiety—is getting through it with Christ.

---

*Lord, I'm so nervous about this situation and not sure
I can make it. Thank You for reminding me that I can
do all things because You give me the strength! Amen.*

A Feathered Reminder

"Are not five sparrows sold for two pennies? And not one of them is forgotten before God. . . . Fear not; you are of more value than many sparrows."

LUKE 12:6–7 ESV

Sparrows were cheap—less than a penny each!—in Jesus' day. We don't think much of these birds now either, if we think of them at all. Yet the Bible says that every single sparrow is thought of by God. More than that, they are in His care: "Not one of them will fall to the ground apart from [Him]" (Matthew 10:29 ESV). God sees and intervenes in the lives of creatures that aren't even made in His image, so it's certain He will go above and beyond that attention in our lives. When you're anxious, look to the birds, and remember God's word to you: "Fear not; you are of more value than many sparrows."

Lord, may I never doubt that I am valued by You and that You care for me. Amen.

Why Be Anxious?

"Which of you by being anxious can add a single hour to his span of life? If then you are not able to do as small a thing as that, why are you anxious about the rest?"

LUKE 12:25-26 ESV

Maybe there's still a part of you that thinks worrying has some benefit. Believe the Son of God when He says worrying is useless: if worrying won't add one hour to our life span, it's not going to change the state of our lives or the state of the world.

Had Jesus ended there, not worrying would have a bitter edge to it. *Why worry? We're stuck with the way things are.* But Jesus finished with *reassurance*: God clothes the lilies in splendor—He's got us covered too (vv. 27-28). God sees our needs—and He sees to it that our needs are met (vv. 29-31).

Lord, You say, "Don't worry," not just because worrying won't achieve anything but because You're already handling my cares. Thank You. Amen.

Let It Reign!

Let the peace of Christ rule in your hearts, since as members of one body you were called to peace.
COLOSSIANS 3:15 NIV

Does anxiety reign in your heart most days? Anxiety is a tyrant. Once we let it in a little, it takes a lot. It isn't content with a corner of our hearts—it usurps every square inch, places that should be filled with peace and joy.

Colossians 3:15 tells us that peace is something we *let* rule in our hearts. It says to "*let* the peace of Christ *have power over your hearts*" (NLV, italics added). We want peace not anxiety, but do we ever block peace by letting anxiety dominate us? By letting anxious thoughts go unchecked? By letting old wounds fester? By letting Satan's lies become our truth? . . . Oust that anxiety! Let God's peace reign instead.

Lord, where am I letting anxiety rule?
Help me make way for Your peace. Amen.

Peace of the Spirit

The fruit of the Spirit is love, joy, peace, forbearance,
kindness, goodness, faithfulness, gentleness and
self-control. Against such things there is no law.
GALATIANS 5:22-23 NIV

Peace isn't something we come by naturally. Peace isn't something we create. Peace is a fruit of the Spirit. But what does that mean?

When we believe in Jesus, God sends His Holy Spirit into our hearts, and His presence changes what's produced in our lives. Where before the flesh produced sin, the Spirit now produces godly characteristics. Traits like love, joy, and peace.

So it's not up to us to manufacture peace. Still, if we want to see the fullness of Spirit-produced peace, we must "walk by the Spirit"; we must "keep in step" with Him (Galatians 5:16, 25 NIV). Anytime our peace is in short supply, we should check ourselves: Are we walking solo?

Lord, walking without You isn't working. I need
You! Guide me back in step with You. Amen.

Near to Us

*Let your gentleness be evident to all. The Lord
is near. Do not be anxious about anything.*

PHILIPPIANS 4:5–6 NIV

It's a big, big world. Our earth is almost twenty-five thousand miles around at the equator. We're among billions of people who call this planet home. We could get lost in that bigness. . .like a thimble swept into the sea. No wonder we feel anxious at times.

But notice what Paul wrote before "Do not be anxious": "The Lord is near." Our ability to not worry begins (and ends) with that truth—God is near. It's not us against the world. God is near. We're not alone or unseen. God is near. Our burdens aren't left to us to carry. God is near. We don't have to rely on ourselves. God is near. The world is a big, big place, but God is near.

---

*Lord, You are near! And because You
are near, I will not be anxious. Amen.*

Plans

In their hearts humans plan their course,
but the Lord establishes their steps.
PROVERBS 16:9 NIV

If you're a live-day-by-day person, maybe plans going awry don't cause you much anxiety. But if you're a planner—an everything's-mapped-out person—then things not going as planned can be a source of intense anxiety.

Some might read Proverbs 16:9 and label God domineering: We plan, only to have God override our plans in favor of His. Or we could read this verse and thank God for helping us. We can't see into the future; we don't always know what's best. God can see and does know. And He keeps us on the right track: "The mind of a man plans his way, but the Lord shows him what to do" (Proverbs 16:9 NLV). Let's not sweat changes to our plans but trust that God is guiding us.

Lord, having a plan makes me less anxious,
but I won't worry no matter how things
go. I will work on trusting You. Amen.

A Message for Anxious Hearts

*Strengthen the weak hands, and make firm
the feeble knees. Say to those who have an
anxious heart, "Be strong; fear not! Behold,
your God. . . . He will come and save you."*

ISAIAH 35:3–4 ESV

Anxiety is nothing new. Even before the complexities of modern society, people felt uneasy about the future. And even back then, God did not wish His people to be anxious.

God sent Isaiah to prophesy judgment and oppression. He promised hard times ahead, but that was only part of the message. There was also hope. "Steady those who are quaking," Isaiah said, "and tell those who are anxious to hold on". . .because God was on the way. He would not allow them to endure hard times forever.

What a message for us today! Repeat it to yourself—or share it with someone else who has an anxious heart.

Lord, thank You for Your Word of hope. Amen.

Given to God

*Give your way over to the Lord. Trust in Him
also. And He will do it. He will make your
being right and good show as the light.*
PSALM 37:5-6 NLV

If we're going on vacation, we'd prefer a good weather forecast. If we're running late for work, we'd prefer green lights . . . . In most situations, we have some preference. The same goes whether we're planning a business venture, hoping to start a family, searching for an apartment—you name it. We want A to happen. . .so we try to control the outcome, which makes us anxious, or we become worried that B (an unwanted outcome) will happen instead.

But the Bible says to let go: "Give your way over to the Lord. Trust in Him." Who better to take charge than the One who controls all and wills only the best for us?

---

*Lord, I need to give this situation to You. Today,
I'm resolving to trust You with the outcome. Amen.*

Quiet Strength

The Lord God, the Holy One of Israel,
has said, "In turning away from sin and in
rest, you will be saved. Your strength will
come by being quiet and by trusting."

ISAIAH 30:15 NLV

Jesus once said that to enter God's kingdom, we must be childlike (Matthew 18:3)—humble and trusting. To experience God's peace, we must be no different. People who insist on doing things their own way in their own strength will find no reason for confidence (Isaiah 30:16).

It's a whole other story if we seek strength "in quietness and trust" (Isaiah 30:15 NIV), if we turn to our Father. Then we can have peace of mind. Isaiah wrote: "The Lord [earnestly] waits [expecting, looking, and longing] to be gracious to you. . . . Blessed. . .are all those who [earnestly] wait for Him. . .[for His victory, His favor, His love, His peace]" (Isaiah 30:18 AMPC).

Lord, only You could turn quietness into strength, fear
of You into fearlessness. Help me rest and trust. Amen.

Permanent Help

"I am sending you out as sheep in the midst
of wolves. . . . When they deliver you over,
do not be anxious how you are to speak
or what you are to say, for what you are
to say will be given to you in that hour."
MATTHEW 10:16, 19 ESV

Picture Jesus standing in front of you. He tells you He's
sending you on a mission where you'll be hated and hurt and
handed over to the courts. He says you'll be a sheep among
wolves. Are you anxious just thinking about such a prospect?
That scene in your head was real for the apostles. So what
did Jesus do? He reminded them not to be worried! God
would provide the words. God would be present always, "even
to the end of the world" (Matthew 28:20 NLV).

Wherever the Lord sends us and whatever we face, we
have that same promise.

Lord, life is frightening sometimes. But I'll remember
that You won't leave me alone for one moment. Amen.

God of Peace

For God is not a God of confusion but of peace.
1 CORINTHIANS 14:33 ESV

Which is better? One person speaking at a time or everyone talking at once? Obviously, if we want to be productive and not have a headache, taking turns is better. Paul shared similar advice with the church in Corinth. His ending argument for orderly gatherings was God not being a God of confusion but of peace.

Our lives can feel like a roomful of clashing voices. Everything happening at once. Nothing making sense. No time to take a breath. In a word: confusion. With God's help, though, our lives can be peaceful. The King James Version translates 1 Corinthians 14:33 as "God is not the author of confusion, but of peace." God is the originator, the creator, of peace. He may not change our circumstances, but if we ask and then let Him, He will hush our inner chaos with His peace.

---

*Lord of peace, Lord of my life, replace
this confusion with peace. Amen.*

Tomorrow's Worries Covered

"Do not be anxious about tomorrow,
for tomorrow will be anxious for itself."
MATTHEW 6:34 ESV

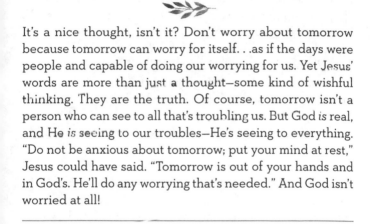

It's a nice thought, isn't it? Don't worry about tomorrow because tomorrow can worry for itself. . .as if the days were people and capable of doing our worrying for us. Yet Jesus' words are more than just a thought—some kind of wishful thinking. They are the truth. Of course, tomorrow isn't a person who can see to all that's troubling us. But God *is* real, and He *is* seeing to our troubles—He's seeing to everything. "Do not be anxious about tomorrow; put your mind at rest," Jesus could have said. "Tomorrow is out of your hands and in God's. He'll do any worrying that's needed." And God isn't worried at all!

Lord, I worry a lot about tomorrow. Help me not be
anxious. Help me remember that You've taken care
of tomorrow and every tomorrow after that. Amen.

Sufficient Troubles

"Sufficient for the day is its own trouble."
MATTHEW 6:34 ESV

As teenage girls, we might have borrowed our friends' clothes. As grown-up women, we might still borrow from our friends. In either case, we generally borrow something we *want*. So why on earth would we borrow *trouble*?

When we worry, we make life harder than necessary. Before anything has even happened, we live as if all kinds of inconveniences and catastrophes will take place, and we're no better off for it. Have we been borrowing trouble from tomorrow? Let's give it back. Let's leave tomorrow's trouble where it belongs. And let's live today.

Jesus saying, "Sufficient for the day is its own trouble," may not be our favorite verse, right along with "In this world you will have trouble" (John 16:33 NIV). Still, they're words we shouldn't skim over. In each day we will have trouble, yes. . . but each day's trouble is quite enough.

Lord, walk with me through this day, through these troubles. Tomorrow can wait. Amen.

First Seek

"Do not worry, saying, 'What shall we eat?' or
'What shall we drink?' or 'What shall we wear?'
For the pagans run after all these things, and
your heavenly Father knows that you need them.
But seek first his kingdom and his righteousness,
and all these things will be given to you as well."

MATTHEW 6:31–33 NIV

Some of us have selective brains. For instance, we might read
Matthew 6:31-33 and see the parts about our heavenly Father
knowing our needs and Him giving to us. The parts about
pagans and God's kingdom are just transitions in between.
If we're struggling with anxiety, though, maybe we're missing
the transitions.

We can't live like "people who do not know God" (v. 32
NLV) and expect not to worry. We must seek God and "be
right with Him" (v. 33 NLV) if we want peace about everything
else. So today, focus on those transitions—and trust God
with the rest.

Lord, help me put You first so that peace will follow. Amen.

Silencer of Storms

Then they cried out to the LORD in their trouble, and he brought them out of their distress. He stilled the storm to a whisper; the waves of the sea were hushed.

PSALM 107:28–29 NIV

It's a beautiful, sunny day. . .until the clouds begin to gather. The sky darkens to a grumpy gray. A storm is rolling in. Pretty soon, wind lashes the trees and rain pelts the ground.

Things can go from fair to stormy in our lives as quickly. One minute we're doing fine, and the next minute we're trying desperately to wait out the trials. But every storm, no matter how intense, obeys the voice of our Lord, the One who "rebuked the wind" and "the wind died down" (Mark 4:39 NIV). And any storm, whether external or internal, can be subdued with His words: "Peace! Be still!" (Mark 4:39 ESV).

If only we cry out to Him.

Lord, please quiet this storm—inside and out. Amen.

A Good, Hard Look

Search me, God, and know my heart;
test me and know my anxious thoughts
. . . . Lead me in the way everlasting.
PSALM 139:23–24 NIV

One tactic for dealing with anxious thoughts is to ignore them. To push them aside without really addressing them. While this might sound good—as if we're choosing not to dwell on anxious thoughts—it might not be good. Like sin that we must recognize before we can be rid of it, we need to identify our anxious thoughts. We need to drag them into the light. That's not easy. That's why the psalmist reached out to God. And that's why we should too. *Search me. Know my anxious thoughts* can be our prayer. Then, with everything out in the open, we can be led "in the way everlasting." We can be guided along "ancient paths, where the good way is . . . and find rest" (Jeremiah 6:16 ESV).

Lord, look into my heart, at all my anxious
thoughts, and lead me Your way. Amen.

Worried Sick

For you created my inmost being; you knit me together in my mother's womb. I praise you because I am fearfully and wonderfully made; your works are wonderful, I know that full well. . . . Your eyes saw my unformed body; all the days ordained for me were written in your book before one of them came to be.

PSALM 139:13–14, 16 NIV

The One who formed our bodies and our days knows *exactly* what's going on inside us. So when we're worried about our health—that freckle looking weird, or the abnormal results to a routine test, or a symptom we just can't shake—the Great Physician is on call. He can apply balm to our fears as we wait for the appointment, for the test results. He has our lives in His hands. And He won't leave our side whether the prognosis is good or bad.

Lord, this concern may be something or nothing. Let's talk, Lord. Let me rest in You. . . . Amen.

Now, Not Later

*"Give your entire attention to what God
is doing right now, and don't get worked up
about what may or may not happen tomorrow."*
MATTHEW 6:34 MSG

Kids wanna grow up. Teenagers can't wait to be adults. Grown-ups look forward to the next big thing. . . . Anticipating "tomorrow" isn't always negative. But when we look ahead and see hardship, anticipation quickly turns to anxiety.

We can't know the future, much less live it out in the present, so Jesus encourages us to be present dwellers. Instead of becoming unsettled over "what may or may not happen tomorrow," we're to settle ourselves in "what God is doing right now." God is working in this moment, and we might miss it if our mind's eye is glued on moments we can't actually see. But if we're here with God, moment by moment, we won't miss a thing—except anxiety.

---

*Lord, I do get worked up about the future. My mind
rushes ahead. Help me stay present with You. Amen.*

Watch. Pray.

"Watch and pray so that you will not fall into temptation. The spirit is willing, but the flesh is weak."
MATTHEW 26:41 NIV

Jesus took His closest companions with Him to Gethsemane and asked one thing of them: "Keep watch with me" (Matthew 26:38 NIV). Maybe it had been a hot day, and then there was the wine they drank at supper. . .their eyelids grew heavy. They did the opposite of what Jesus had asked—they fell asleep (v. 40). We might try to deny it, but how like the disciples we are!

Over and over God asks us to stop worrying and trust Him. And over and over we do the opposite. We *want* to do as He says, but our human nature is weak. How can we not trip over ourselves, then? By being proactive. By asking God to guard our hearts and grow our trust. By watching and praying.

---

*Lord, keep watch with me. Help
me not fall into worries. Amen.*

Healed of Worry

Wherever he went—into villages, towns or countryside—they placed the sick in the marketplaces. They begged him to let them touch even the edge of his cloak, and all who touched it were healed.

MARK 6:56 NIV

There were no cell phones, but word somehow traveled fast one day in Gennesaret. Jesus had barely stepped ashore, and the people knew it: "As soon as [Jesus and His disciples] got out of the boat, people recognized Jesus. They ran throughout that whole region and carried the sick on mats to wherever they heard he was" (Mark 6:54-55 NIV). No dawdling here. These men and women made tracks. They hustled to the Healer.

Do we do the same? We're often sick with worry. We come down with cases of fear and doubt. Let's *run* to God's presence, sure that a single touch will heal our hearts.

Lord, I've been suffering with this anxiety, trying to handle it on my own, when I need to run to You. I need Your healing. Amen.

The Sleep of the Trusting

I will lie down and sleep in peace.
O Lord, You alone keep me safe.
PSALM 4:8 NLV

The stress of the day could have you so revved up that you can't slow down to rest. Worries could wake you in the middle of the night and nag your mind till dawn. Sleep that was so natural when you were a baby, a kid, can suddenly become complex as an adult. If anxiety is keeping you awake, it's not sleep hygiene that needs to be addressed. It's your heart.

In Psalm 4, the psalmist—David—credited his peaceful sleep to God. He gave the same reason for secure, sound sleep in Psalm 3, which he wrote while fleeing from Absalom: "I lay down and slept, and I woke up again, for the Lord keeps me safe" (v. 5 NLV).

Why are you anxious? Ask God's help in handing over those worries, in putting your trust in Him.

Take my worries, Lord. Please give
me sleep, for I trust You. Amen.

For Us

What can we say about all these things?
Since God is for us, who can be against us?
ROMANS 8:31 NLV

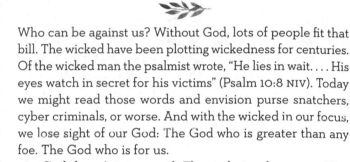

Who can be against us? Without God, lots of people fit that bill. The wicked have been plotting wickedness for centuries. Of the wicked man the psalmist wrote, "He lies in wait. . . . His eyes watch in secret for his victims" (Psalm 10:8 NIV). Today we might read those words and envision purse snatchers, cyber criminals, or worse. And with the wicked in our focus, we lose sight of our God: The God who is greater than any foe. The God who is for us.

God doesn't ignore evil. The psalmist also wrote, "But You [God] have seen it. You look upon trouble and suffering, to take it into Your hands" (Psalm 10:14 NLV). We can commit ourselves to God's care. There is no better advocate, no better ally, than He.

Lord, when I'm anxious about who's against
me, remind me that You are for me. Amen.

Set on the Spirit

*For to set the mind on the flesh is death, but to
set the mind on the Spirit is life and peace.*
ROMANS 8:6 ESV

If Peter Pan wanted to fly, he needed two things: pixie dust and a happy thought. Not a grumpy, angry, or worried thought. A happy one. To think any other thought meant remaining ground-bound, despite buckets of pixie dust.

The Bible says that "to set the mind on the flesh is death, but to set the mind on the Spirit is life and peace." Simple enough. Yet we struggle to get it through our heads that what occupies our thoughts also preoccupies our hearts. If we spend our waking hours obsessing over earthly things, catering to our every whim and desire, is it any wonder that anxiety weighs us down? But if instead we think Spirit-thoughts, then the binds are broken, and we are lifted into life and peace.

---

*Lord, I need help with this. Help me
set my mind on the Spirit. Amen.*

Thoughts Taken in Hand

We break down every thought and proud thing that puts itself up against the wisdom of God. We take hold of every thought and make it obey Christ.

2 Corinthians 10:5 nlv

Paul's directives were never wimpy or passive. Take 2 Corinthians 10:5. We're not told to give thoughts a glance or a halfhearted push to the back of our minds. We're told to "take hold of" a thought—grab it, seize it. Then we are to "make it obey"—force it to fall in line. And which thoughts? Every one.

Every thought—whether its source is self or someone else—should be compared and conformed to God's wisdom. So when a thought says, "Be afraid," we look to scripture that says, "Fear not." When a thought says, "Time to panic," we look to scripture that says, "God is faithful." And so on and so on until every anxious thought gives way beneath peace.

Lord, sometimes what enters my mind doesn't line up with Your truth. May every thought become obedient to You. Amen.

Escapable

God is faithful; he will not let you be tempted beyond what you can bear. But when you are tempted, he will also provide a way out so that you can endure it.

1 CORINTHIANS 10:13 NIV

In some situations, worry seems inescapable: A loved one is sick or injured, and it's critical. Wars are declared. We're faced with a hurricane, flood, or fire. . . . Then you might say in your heart, "How can I help but worry?" You might even take your worry to the extreme: "How can I trust a God who lets this happen?"

In situations where we're tempted to give in to our worries and give up trusting God, He is still faithful. In times of testing, God makes it possible for us to endure. In trials, God grants us peace that "passeth all understanding" (Philippians 4:7 KJV). Worry is never inescapable when God provides the way out.

Lord, show me the way out of my worries. Amen.

God beyond Measure

Now to him who is able to do immeasurably more
than all we ask or imagine, according to his power
that is at work within us, to him be glory.
EPHESIANS 3:20–21 NIV

We've heard the stories of our miracle-working God—stories like God parting the Red Sea and protecting Shadrach, Meshach, and Abednego from a red-hot furnace. Or the times Jesus healed the sick and raised the dead. Through those stories, we learn the truth that God has no limitations and meets with no impossibilities.

That same truth can change our entire outlook when we're anxious.

Nothing we're anxious about falls outside God's power to upend, redirect, or quash. God can, in fact, do "immeasurably more" than anything we think. And even if He doesn't alter our circumstances, He will transform us in ways that far surpass our hopes and expectations. After all, He is our miracle-working God.

I ask for peace, Lord, but I pray too for faith
that You're capable of much, much more! Amen.

Keep On

*And let us not grow weary of doing good, for in
due season we will reap, if we do not give up.*

GALATIANS 6:9 ESV

The Bible promises good for good. When we serve and obey God, our efforts are never wasted. We may not see the harvest right away—or even in this life—but there will be a harvest.

Learning to be peaceful and not anxious is a weary process at times. We determine to do one thing—trust; we end up doing another—worry. We think we're making progress, only to backtrack. We grow tired when the worries won't let up.

If you're in that weary spot today, hear the Spirit whisper, *"Keep going."* Keep addressing anxiety. Keep seeking God's help day by day, hour by hour when it's tough. In due season you will reap His reward if you do not give up.

*Lord, reenergize me. I'm not settling for
anything less than Your peace. Amen.*

Peace to You

*Suddenly a great company of the heavenly host
appeared with the angel, praising God and saying,
"Glory to God in the highest heaven, and on
earth peace to those on whom his favor rests."*

LUKE 2:13-14 NIV

The night was ordinary. The same stars filled the sky. The same sheep filled the pasture. The shepherds were out watching the flocks, as they did every night. The night *was* ordinary; then an angel appeared, filling the space around them with God's glory and delivering an extraordinary message: Peace on earth. Peace with God.

We might think of the shepherds' story only once a year. It's a story told against a backdrop of tinsel and lights. But that message that was first delivered on an ordinary night is a message for any old day. It's a message that meets us wherever we are–whatever the backdrop of our lives—and reminds us that we've been given peace.

*Lord, may I carry Your message of
peace in my heart every day. Amen.*

Blessed Are We

Blessed is the people of whom this is true;
blessed is the people whose God is the LORD.
PSALM 144:15 NIV

"Take me out of trouble," David asked of God (Psalm 144:7, 11 NLV). He looked forward to a day of deliverance—a day that would lead to blessings: "Then our sons in their youth will be like well-nurtured plants, and our daughters will be like pillars carved to adorn a palace. Our barns will be filled. . . . Our sheep will increase by thousands. . . . There will be no breaching of walls, no going into captivity, no cry of distress in our streets" (vv. 12-14 NIV).

Still today, we look forward to deliverance from troubles. We hope to say we are blessed because good has befallen us. *But* should tragedy upon tragedy be heaped on us instead, we are still blessed. We are infinitely better off and eternally blessed because our God is the Lord.

Lord, why am I so anxious when I am so blessed? Amen.

Numbered Days

So teach us to number our days, that we
may apply our hearts unto wisdom.
PSALM 90:12 KJV

It's a familiar adage: Life is short. We're not guaranteed long years on this planet, but even if we live to be a hundred and twenty, our lives are brief. Mere specks in time. Here today, gone too soon. James put it this way: "What is your life? You are a mist that appears for a little while and then vanishes" (James 4:14 NIV).

For the Christian, who has eternity in heaven ahead, life's brevity isn't a cause for lost hope or panic; still, it should motivate us to use this time well. "Teach us to number our days," the psalmist wrote. Why? "That we may apply our hearts unto wisdom." Regardless of how many years God allots us, would we want to waste *any* of our days worrying when we could be gaining a heart that knows how to live wisely?

Lord, teach me to number my days. Amen.

Believe

"Let not your hearts be troubled.
Believe in God; believe also in me."

JOHN 14:1 ESV

Jesus told His followers not to have troubled hearts. He then presented the antithesis of worry: belief. Jesus was real—the disciples could actually see and touch Him. What's more, Jesus could be believed. He would keep His promises: "If it were not so, would I have told you that I go to prepare a place for you? And if I go and prepare a place for you, I will come again and will take you to myself" (John 14:2-3 ESV).

God is real. We cannot see Him, but in our hearts we know it's true; in our world we witness the truth (see Romans 1:19-20). And God can be believed! He has never reneged and never will.

Do you believe in Him? Do not let your heart be troubled.

"Don't worry. Believe." Lord, believing doesn't seem like it's enough. But belief in You—God Almighty—is a powerful thing! Amen.

Holy Comforter

And I will pray the Father, and he shall
give you another Comforter, that he
may abide with you for ever.

JOHN 14:16 KJV

Your alarm clock goes off. It's time to start another day. Now, if the day ahead is sunshiny, you might get right up and get going. But if the day has worries filling your mind like storm clouds, you might want to hide under the blankets instead, to sink deep into the comfort of your bed rather than deal with those worries.

What if you could somehow bring comfort with you into your day? You can, of course! John 14:16 tells you so. Jesus knew we would head into many cloudy days, so He prayed that Father God would send a Comforter. From then on the Holy Spirit would dwell in us, and we would not be left comfortless—ever (see John 14:17–18 KJV).

Lord, thank You for the Spirit.
Thank You for comfort. Amen.

Holy Helper

"The Helper is the Holy Spirit. The Father will send Him in My place. He will teach you everything and help you remember everything I have told you."

JOHN 14:26 NLV

Were the Holy Spirit to do only one thing—comfort—that would still be a wondrous thing. But the Spirit's work in us goes beyond that. Another ministry of the Spirit is to help us. And who couldn't use *lots* of help in days of worry?

The prophet Isaiah described the Spirit that would rest on Christ as "the Spirit of wisdom and of understanding, the Spirit of counsel and of might, the Spirit of the knowledge and fear of the LORD" (Isaiah 11:2 NIV). Think of it: that same Spirit dwells in us!

Whatever our need, just as the disciples turned to Jesus, the One who walked beside them, we can turn to the Spirit who lives inside us.

Lord, thank You for Your Spirit's help. Amen.

This Day

Our Father which art in heaven, Hallowed be thy name. Thy kingdom come, Thy will be done in earth, as it is in heaven. Give us this day our daily bread.

MATTHEW 6:9–11 KJV

The Lord's Prayer (Matthew 6:9–13) may be so familiar that we breeze through the words. But tucked in the middle is a statement that teaches our anxious hearts about trust: "Give us this day our daily bread." Jesus was asking our Father to provide, yet His request wasn't "Give us everything we'll ever need" but "Give us *this* day our *daily* bread." In other words, meet our needs for today. By asking for this day's needs, we train our hearts to stay in the present and not rush ahead to future days. We train our hearts to trust, day by day, the God who promises to take care of us all our days.

Lord, it seems like I'm always thinking ahead. Keep me in today. Care for and keep me this day. Amen.

A Lesson from Esther

[Mordecai] had brought up Hadassah, that is Esther.
ESTHER 2:7 NLV

Esther was queen "for such a time as this" (Esther 4:14 NIV)—and what a time, with such potential to worry! Esther had gone from an unknown girl to the king's favorite; now her cousin wanted her to help save the Jews. That's daunting enough, but Esther's intervention was risky too. Her life would be at stake.

Yet once Esther decided to help, she didn't burst into the king's court to get it over with. She asked the people to fast. She fasted. For three days. Three *long* days with her and the Jews' fate up in the air. We're not given details about those days, but by the end of them, Esther was ready.

We face situations where the outcome is uncertain to us. But nothing is ever uncertain to God. And when we prepare ourselves in His presence, we will be ready for anything.

Lord, steady me, ready me,
for whatever times I face. Amen.

A Lesson from Ruth

*[Naomi] was left with her two sons. They married
Moabite women, one named Orpah and the other Ruth.*
RUTH 1:3-4 NIV

Given the choice, would you rather remain in familiar circumstances—with familiar relatives and culture—or travel miles and miles away—away from your relatives and your culture? Ruth chose the latter. Her husband had died, and her widowed mother-in-law was returning to her hometown of Bethlehem. Even though Naomi urged Ruth to go back to Moab, Ruth's homeland, Ruth refused: "Where you go I will go, and where you stay I will stay" (Ruth 1:16 NIV).

If Ruth was anxious, she didn't show it. That kind of determination was only possible because there was a third member of the traveling group: God. "Your God will be my God," Ruth told Naomi (Ruth 1:16 NLV). It was faith in God that sustained Ruth—and eventually rewarded her.

---

*Lord, may I boldly face the unfamiliar
because You are my God. Amen.*

Rock of the Aging

"Even when you are old I will be the same.
And even when your hair turns white, I will
help you. I will take care of what I have
made. I will carry you, and will save you."

Isaiah 46:4 NLV

Does anyone like the idea of getting older? Thoughts about aging aren't always peaceful, especially if we're worried about finances, poor health, or being left alone in our golden years.

How can we stop worried thoughts in their tracks? It isn't by convincing ourselves (or *trying* to convince ourselves) that a retirement account will support us, that good genes will help us, or that kids or grandkids will be there for us. It's by reminding ourselves that though we age, God is eternal. And it's by repeating His promise: "I will carry. I will help. I will be there to see you through."

Lord, help me trust in You to take
care of me my whole life. Amen.

Not Impossible

For with God nothing is ever impossible
and no word from God shall be without
power or impossible of fulfillment.

LUKE 1:37 AMPC

"With God nothing is ever impossible." Nothing impossible.
Nothing. The reality of Luke 1:37 might be difficult for us to
imagine. So much from our perspective seems impossible:
The way ahead is blocked. We've run out of solutions. Our
hands are tied. . . . It's easy to worry when we see things from
our perspective. That's when we need God's perspective.
That's when we need to repeat Luke 1:37 until we believe it!
"With God nothing is ever impossible." No way blocked. No
solution-less scenario. No hands tied. . .no impossibilities.

What has you worried today? Take a breath. And face
reality: "With God nothing is ever impossible."

Lord, I'm worried. This situation I'm in—well, it seems
impossible that it will turn out all right. But You
make things possible. Help me trust You. Amen.

Ousted Worry

Don't fret or worry. Instead of worrying,
pray. Let petitions and praises shape your
worries into prayers, letting God know your
concerns. Before you know it, a sense of
God's wholeness, everything coming together
for good, will come and settle you down.
It's wonderful what happens when Christ
displaces worry at the center of your life.
PHILIPPIANS 4:6–7 MSG

When worry is the center of your days, it might seem too simplistic—this idea that praying instead of worrying will turn an anxious heart into a settled heart. But it's true. Truly! We can't comprehend *how* it happens, but we still experience it happening. That's why this verse calls it wonderful. God's peace is a wonder; it's a peace that "surpasses all understanding" (Philippians 4:7 ESV). And it comes simply with talking to God instead of worrying. With letting "a sense of God's wholeness" enter. With seeing Christ become the center of every day.

With each prayer, Lord, center my
heart in You and Your peace. Amen.

Peace Restored

*But the God of all grace, who hath called
us unto his eternal glory by Christ Jesus,
after that ye have suffered a while, make
you perfect, stablish, strengthen, settle you.*

1 PETER 5:10 KJV

Although it's possible to be peaceless anytime (we could have a picture-perfect life and yet have no peace), times of suffering tend to unsettle us more than the good times. Suffering stretches us to our limits, and it so often drains our peace in the process. We long for trials to end so peace can return. We crave the blessed hush after the storm has passed.

God is able to give us internal peace regardless of what's happening around us. But we also have His word that He will restore us to a place of peace after the suffering ends. Then God Himself will make us all the better, all the more peaceful.

---

*Lord, be my peace through this suffering until,
in only a little while, You will stablish,
strengthen, settle me. Amen.*

Cause for Laughter

She is clothed with strength and dignity;
she can laugh at the days to come.
PROVERBS 31:25 NIV

Think back to a time when you were anxious. With a heart full of worry, fear, and dread, chances are you weren't contemplating the days ahead and laughing (unless perhaps the laughter served as a dam to keep the tears from gushing). Contrast your experience with the example woman of Proverbs 31: "She can laugh at the days to come."

Now, we might think of the Proverbs 31 woman as "perfect." But whatever *her* qualities, you can bet the circumstances of her life would not be perfect. No one is exempt from hardship and stress, uncertainty and disappointment. There's another reason for her bubbly confidence. It's the backbone behind all her praiseworthy qualities—"fear of the Lord" (v. 30). The woman who lives in awe of the Almighty needn't fear anything else.

Lord of my life, because of You, I can look
ahead with confidence, with laughter. Amen.

"I've Got You"

"That's right. Because I, your GOD, have a firm
grip on you and I'm not letting go. I'm telling
you, 'Don't panic. I'm right here to help you.'"
ISAIAH 41:13 MSG

The training wheels were coming off today, and the little
girl was excited to ride her big-girl bike. She was a tiny bit
nervous once she started pedaling down the sidewalk, but
she remembered that her daddy was running along behind
her with his strong hand holding on to the seat. Eventually,
though, the father let go, and the girl looked back. Panic set
in as she realized she was riding all alone.

Living life is more complicated than riding a bike. But
we can be sure of this: There will never be a moment that
we look back and don't see our Father holding the seat. For
not a single pump of the pedals will He leave us without His
steadying grip.

Lord, thank You for being near,
not far, right here with me. Amen.

Welfare and Peace

*For I know the thoughts and plans that I
have for you, says the Lord, thoughts and
plans for welfare and peace and not for evil,
to give you hope in your final outcome.*

JEREMIAH 29:11 AMPC

When life is going swimmingly, it's easy to believe verses like Jeremiah 29:11. But what about when life isn't going so well? What about times when we splash and struggle and barely keep afloat? It's easy then to feel as if God is out to get us.

No matter what our circumstances seem to say, we must have faith in what God actually says—that He's thinking about us, that He has plans for us and those thoughts and plans are *good*. Stuck in our present, we can't see the end, but we can trust God along the way. We can trust Him for our welfare and peace.

*Lord, I'm anxious about the future, but You
give me hope. Help me relax, however
You choose to work things out. Amen.*

Forward Lookers

*Keep your eyes on Jesus, who both began
and finished this race we're in. Study how he
did it. Because he never lost sight of where
he was headed—that exhilarating finish in
and with God—he could put up with anything
along the way: Cross, shame, whatever.*

HEBREWS 12:2 MSG

The author of Hebrews used a footrace as an analogy for life. To you, life might not feel like a race but a long, arduous journey. Either way, if we lose sight of our destination, we might also lose the will to go on. We might become so upset by the stresses that moving forward, even just one step, seems too much.

Let's take our eyes off our weary feet and the obstacles all around and instead keep our eyes on Jesus. Let's keep looking toward "that exhilarating finish"!

---

*I can put up with any worrisome thing if You
help me keep my eyes on You, Lord, and
the joy You've led the way to. Amen.*

Built on the Rock

*"Therefore everyone who hears these words of
mine and puts them into practice is like a wise
man who built his house on the rock. The rain
came down, the streams rose, and the winds blew
and beat against that house; yet it did not fall,
because it had its foundation on the rock."*

MATTHEW 7:24-25 NIV

During His earthly ministry, Jesus told us how to live forever
and also how to live now. If we want to live wisely—soundly—
we'll listen to Jesus' words and follow them. To build our
lives on anything other than His Word is like a house on
sand. Insecure. Jostled by every shift. Prone to collapsing.
But when our foundation is on the Rock? All kinds of stresses
can come our way, and although we feel their presence, we
don't budge.

*Lord, I'm good at hearing Your words; help me be
as good at putting them into practice. I want to
feel grounded through every stress. Amen.*

God, Our Caretaker

*Casting the whole of your care [all your
anxieties, all your worries, all your concerns,
once and for all] on Him, for He cares for you
affectionately and cares about you watchfully.*
1 PETER 5:7 AMPC

Got a lot of worries? God wants them. The whole caboodle.
For keeps. You see, our worries are no burden to Him.

But the Bible's instruction to cast the entirety of our
cares on God isn't given only because He can handle our
worries, whereas we can't. We're told to cast our cares on
God because He cares. God "cares for you affectionately
and cares about you watchfully." And to think, this is God
Almighty we're talking about! The One who created and rules
the world cares affectionately and watchfully.

Why hold on to our worries for even one millisecond
when a God like that calls us His own, calls us to cast our
cares on Him?

Every worry, Lord, I'm casting on You. Amen.

Content in His Care

*So be content with who you are. . . . God's strong
hand is on you; he'll promote you at the right time.
Live carefree before God; he is most careful with you.*

1 PETER 5:6–7 MSG

A friend posts an enviable life update. A girl from college is
way ahead of you career-wise. That celebrity always looks
so perfect. And suddenly you're discontent and anxiously
thinking about ways to be more like somebody else. Stupid
posts! Stupid pictures! But the source of that kind of stress
really isn't outside us; it's in ourselves.

God is sovereign over our lives, and that's a wonderful
thought—provided we get to the headspace where we trust
Him to know what He's doing. Then it doesn't matter what
our lives are like compared to anyone else's. We can say with
confidence in God's plan, "His hand is on me."

---

*Lord, I create a lot of stress by not being
content with myself. But today I'm going
to live carefree before You. Amen.*

Out of the Woods

*Through the tender mercy of our God; whereby the
dayspring from on high hath visited us, to give light
to them that sit in darkness and in the shadow of
death, to guide our feet into the way of peace.*

LUKE 1:78–79 KJV

At the beginning of the Disney movie *The Sword in the Stone*,
the audience enters a dark forest. The forest is where threats
lurk, where hardship and fear predominate. That's not a
bad comparison to our lives before knowing Christ. On our
own, we "sit in darkness and in the shadow of death." And
we'd be sitting there even now—but the Dayspring came! He
penetrated the thick canopy and bathed us in His light. He
led our feet out of the forest into the way of peace.

Worries can make us feel as if we're back in the dark
forest. Are you there today? God still gives light, still guides
us to peace.

*Lord, take my heart from worries
to a bright, open space. Amen.*

Not a Moment Too Late

*When they deliver you up, do not be anxious about
how or what you are to speak; for what you are to
say will be given you in that very hour and moment.*
MATTHEW 10:19 AMPC

Corrie ten Boom was a brave woman. She risked everything
to hide Jews in her home during World War II. But years
before, Corrie wondered if she could bravely serve God. As
the story goes, Corrie's father reminded her that whenever
she bought a train ticket, he would give her the money just
before she bought the ticket, not weeks before. She could
depend on God for courage too, at the exact moment she
needed it.

God can give us what we need ahead of time—whether
we need courage (as Corrie did), words (as the disciples
in Matthew 10:19 did), or anything else. Often, though, He
says, "Don't worry. I will meet your need in that very hour
and moment."

*Lord, I trust You. Every moment.
And for every need. Amen.*

Sick with Worries

My sighing is not hidden from you. . . . Lord,
I wait for you; you will answer, Lord my God.
PSALM 38:9, 15 NIV

Worry begins in the heart—but spreads to the body. Who hasn't felt their nervousness in their stomach? Who hasn't grown tired from anxious nights spent awake? Maybe headaches plague our days along with the worries. Maybe stress is stressing every part of us. Maybe Psalm 38:6–8, 10 (KJV) hits close to home: "I am troubled; I am bowed down greatly. . . . There is no soundness in my flesh. I am feeble and sore broken. . . . My heart panteth, my strength faileth me."

Yet even when we are at our worst amid worries, we can hope for—expect—the best. Our struggle is not invisible to God. And in His perfect time, He will answer us.

Lord, I feel this worry head to toe, skin to bone.
Calm my anxious body as I wait for You. Amen.

Thorny Issue

"Still others, like seed sown among thorns, hear the word; but the worries of this life, the deceitfulness of wealth and the desires for other things come in and choke the word, making it unfruitful."

MARK 4:18–19 NIV

If you wanted an example of how destructive worry can be, you would find one in Jesus' parable of the sower. In the parable, the Gospel message is spread like seed over different types of ground—bare, rocky, thorny, and good. The types of ground represent responses to hearing the Gospel. On the thorny soil, the message is choked out by worries. Thorny-soil hearers are so distracted with life today that they ultimately overlook life eternal.

What is our role here—we who have heard the message, received it, and seen the fruit of our decision? Pray. Pray that worries don't stunt the effectiveness of the Gospel in anyone's life, for no worry is as powerful as our God!

---

*Lord, may others hear and receive—
that Your Word may be fruitful. Amen.*

Lord and Watchman

Listen, He Who watches over Israel will not close his eyes or sleep. The Lord watches over you. The Lord is your safe cover at your right hand. The sun will not hurt you during the day and the moon will not hurt you during the night. . . . He will watch over your soul. The Lord will watch over your coming and going, now and forever.

PSALM 121:4–8 NLV

"Worrying prepares me for the worst." "Worrying helps me cover all my bases." We might not actually say things like that, but how often does worrying feel sensible? By worrying, we're not naively skipping through life. No, we've set a watchman over our lives.

Soon, though, we discover that our worry watchman is totally inept. He's also wholly unnecessary. God is already *the* Watchman over our lives. He never sleeps. Nothing escapes His notice. And He does more than sound the alarm. He calls the shots.

Lord, why am I anxious when You watch over me? Amen.

Promises and Worry Don't Mix

God has said, "I will never leave you or
let you be alone." So we can say for sure,
"The Lord is my Helper. I am not afraid
of anything man can do to me."
HEBREWS 13:5–6 NLV

God's promises in the Bible should eliminate anxiety. He has made promises for our present and for our future that should free us from worry. So why is it that we doubt and worry anyway? Maybe His promises seem too good to be true. Perhaps we've seen one too many promises broken by people we really trusted.

We can get from this place of anxiety and doubt to a place of peace and trust. How? We have to know our God as well as His promises. We have to soak up His Word and His presence. We have to ask His Spirit to help weak belief become strong.

Lord, draw me toward peace and trust. Teach my heart
to let go of worry and hold on to Your promises. Amen.

Peace Not Punishment

Among those nations you will find no repose,
no resting place for the sole of your foot. There
the LORD will give you an anxious mind, eyes
weary with longing, and a despairing heart. You
will live in constant suspense, filled with dread
both night and day, never sure of your life.
DEUTERONOMY 28:65–66 NIV

Israel had been warned. If they heeded the command to obey, blessing would result. But if they did not, God would intervene. Not even God's chosen people could go their own way in sin forever. God deserved more and loved them too much for that. So God would scatter the people and send punishment. . .and anxiety would be part of that punishment.

Anxiety really is horrible, never something you want in your life. And you know what? *God doesn't want it there either.* He's ever calling us to obey—knowing that as we follow His ways, His peace accompanies us.

Lord, help me realize the peace
You desire in my life. Amen.

Give and Get

*Give all your cares to the Lord and He will
give you strength. He will never let those
who are right with Him be shaken.*

PSALM 55:22 NLV

Giving one thing in order to get another thing has been a part of human history for a long, long time—from ancient trade routes to kids swapping baseball cards. Just think how different your life would be without exchanges. You put in a hard week's work and you get paid. You shell out cash and you get groceries or your lawn mowed—any number of things—in return.

In Psalm 55:22 we're offered an exchange: "Give all your cares to the Lord and He will give you strength." What a deal! There may be times in life when an exchange isn't fair—we give more than we get. But not in this case. Here we give something we don't even want and get back so much more.

*Lord, I gladly give You my cares for
a strong, unshaken life! Amen.*

Planted by the Water

*"But blessed is the one who trusts in the LORD,
whose confidence is in him. They will be like a
tree planted by the water that sends out its roots
by the stream. It does not fear when heat comes;
its leaves are always green. It has no worries in
a year of drought and never fails to bear fruit."*

JEREMIAH 17:7–8 NIV

A tree needs water. If you were to plant a tree and not water it, the leaves would wither, turning from green to brown. Eventually, you'd have only a carcass of a tree. If that tree had emotions, it would be shaking in its roots.

Life is full of heat and drought—hard times that can cause fear and worry. But like trees planted by a constant source of water, our lives draw living water from God when we put our trust in Him.

---

*My confidence is in You, Lord, come rain or drought.
And that means I don't have to be anxious! Amen.*

Trust Refined

*"If we are thrown into the blazing furnace,
the God we serve is able to deliver us.
. . . But even if he does not. . ."*
DANIEL 3:17–18 NIV

A powerful king says to you, "Bow down and worship this gold statue or be thrown into a fiery furnace. Make your choice!" You may be sure of your choice—that you will worship God alone—but will anxiety get the better of you when you answer?

If you've read Daniel 3, you know that Shadrach, Meshach, and Abednego were asked to choose between false worship and a blazing furnace. They didn't squirm as they answered. They gave no hint of doubt, didn't defend themselves either (v. 16)! They just let it be known that in God they trusted, deliverance or no deliverance. Incredible? Only hearts that have leaned on God from day to day can trust Him even when the days are precarious.

*Lord, each day I feel my anxiety lessening
and my trust in You growing. Amen.*

Unentangled

*No man that warreth entangleth himself with
the affairs of this life; that he may please him
who hath chosen him to be a soldier.*

2 TIMOTHY 2:4 KJV

In 2 Timothy 2:4, Paul compared the Christian's life to a soldier's. The soldier's aim is to please his commander; therefore, he doesn't entangle himself with "the affairs of this life." Similarly, we Christians must not allow life's affairs to divert our attention from pleasing God.

Paul had more to say about living unentangled: "Those who use the things of the world, [should live] as if not engrossed in them. For this world in its present form is passing away. I would like you to be free from concern" (1 Corinthians 7:31–32 NIV). When we're engrossed in worldly things, we often get caught up in worry. We obsess over what's passing, and we neglect what's permanent.

Let's live like God is number one—for so He is!

---

*Lord, help me please You and not
become entangled in worries. Amen.*

Surer Than

*The Lord will always lead you. He will meet the needs
of your soul in the dry times and give strength to
your body. You will be like a garden that has enough
water, like a well of water that never dries up.*

ISAIAH 58:11 NLV

Until we're home in heaven or Jesus returns to set things
right on earth, difficulties are normal. Dry times will come.
Wearying days will too. We needn't be surprised by them.
We needn't worry about them either.

As sure as the dry times and the wearying days is our
Lord's presence in our lives. "He will meet the needs of
your soul in the dry times and give strength to your body."
Despite the driest time, we will never dry up. We will never
be without our God.

So, rest easy, anxious heart.

---

*Lord, You have me covered—body and soul. You are surer
than the difficulties. What peace that gives me! Amen.*

When You're Slipping

When I said, "My foot is slipping," your unfailing love, LORD, supported me. When anxiety was great within me, your consolation brought me joy.

PSALM 94:18–19 NIV

No matter how trusting of the Lord we are, no matter how much our hearts rest in Him, situations can come along and bring us to the slipping point. The psalmist was at that point. His feet were skidding over loose debris. His anxiety was ballooning up inside him.

Maybe you've been to that point before: The diagnosis was so staggering, your legs felt like cooked spaghetti. The news was so overwhelming, you began to lose your footing. Your life took such a blow that anxiety was great within you. Maybe you're there *now*.

In those times, go to God and tell it like it is. "My foot is slipping," the psalmist stated. Frank, not fancy. And as simple as that, God's love supported him. God's consolation brought him joy.

Lord, help me be open with You. Amen.

Blessed with Peace

*"The LORD bless you and keep you; the LORD make
his face shine on you and be gracious to you; the
LORD turn his face toward you and give you peace."*
NUMBERS 6:24–26 NIV

Unbelievers may think of God's commands negatively: when
God commands, He's either telling people to do something
they don't want to do or telling people not to do something
they do want to do.

But God's instruction in Numbers doesn't fit that mindset. Here, God tells Moses how to bless the Israelites (v. 23).
God shares how He desires to bless His people. And who
wouldn't welcome blessings like these: "May the Lord bring
good to you and keep you. May the Lord make His face shine
upon you, and be kind to you. May the Lord show favor toward
you, and give you peace" (Numbers 6:24–26 NLV).

---

*Lord, thank You for blessing me with peace
and with countless other blessings! Amen.*

The Worry Weight

Anxiety weighs down the heart,
but a kind word cheers it up.
PROVERBS 12:25 NIV

An anxious heart could be compared to a kite with a weight tied on its tail. A breeze may blow, but that kite ain't gonna fly! We may want to be lighthearted, but our hearts ain't gonna soar.

But what if someone comes along and cuts the string, releasing the kite from the weight? What if someone comes along and says a kind word, relieving the heart of the worry? It's beautiful when this happens in our lives. Even better? Making it happen in another person's life. God has cheered us through many anxious days. We in turn can cheer up a fellow worrier, just as the Bible says: God "gives us comfort in all our troubles. Then we can comfort other people who have the same troubles" (2 Corinthians 1:4 NLV). Who could use some cheering today?

Lord, I well know what it is to be anxious.
Help me spread Your kind of comfort. Amen.

A Peaceful Effect

The effect of righteousness will be peace, and the result of righteousness, quietness and trust forever.

ISAIAH 32:17 ESV

Easy living would give way to hardship. That was Isaiah's message to the women of Judah. They were complacent, not realizing that soon the city would be desolate, the fields like deserts. *However,* the warning had a promise attached—the promise of God's future kingdom: "It will be this way until the Spirit is poured out upon us from heaven, and the desert becomes a field giving so much fruit, that it seems as if it has many trees. . . . Then my people will live in a place of peace, in safe homes, and in quiet resting places" (Isaiah 32:15, 18 NLV).

Anytime God touches down, things change. His effect is peace, security. And we don't have to wait for that future time. God dwells in our hearts now, and with Him come peace and quietness and trust—forever.

Lord, thank You for Your unending peace. Amen.

The Old Way

The Lord says, "Stand by where the roads cross, and look. Ask for the old paths, where the good way is, and walk in it. And you will find rest for your souls."
JEREMIAH 6:16 NLV

Does it ever seem that with each generation we become more obsessed with the new? The newest trend. The latest technology or app. The most recent advances in medicine and science and knowledge. . . The old ways might have worked for our grandparents or great-grandparents, but we prefer the new ways, thank you!

New isn't always bad. Yet we must be careful—especially regarding spiritual matters. God's Word is straightforward on this. Standing at the crossroads, we're to ask for the old paths. We're to seek the good old ways laid out for us by God and followed faithfully by generation upon generation of believers. These ways aren't trendy or flashy, but they are tried and true. They are where we find rest.

Lord, lead me along the old paths. Amen.

Our Delight

Trouble and anguish have found me out,
but your commandments are my delight.
PSALM 119:143 ESV

What is your delight when worries find you out? God blesses us with diversions when we're stressed and need a break. Maybe for you it's a movie that makes you laugh. Or a hobby where you lose track of the time. Maybe it's a trip to the lake with friends. But imagine if that thing was stripped away. Are you also stripped of delight?

Our true delight must be more reliable than our diversions. What gets us through the troubles must transcend the troubles themselves. For the psalmist, that was God's Word. God's Word can become our delight too. It takes one part willingness and commitment to read the Bible—and two parts help. The Author Himself will guide us to the delights of His Word.

Lord, I want to delight in the Bible more, so I'm setting
aside my favorite diversion for a while. Use this time,
Lord, that Your Word may be my delight. Amen.

Unless the Lord

*Unless the LORD builds the house, the builders
labor in vain. Unless the LORD watches over
the city, the guards stand watch in vain.*
PSALM 127:1 NIV

You might recognize some of Solomon's wisdom from Ecclesiastes in Psalm 127—in particular, the vanity of life. Verse 1 describes the fruitlessness of efforts done sans God: Unless the Lord builds, builders build in vain. Unless the Lord watches, watchmen watch in vain.

We ourselves put much effort into projects. We spend a lot of time guarding our lives. But apart from God, we labor and watch in vain. And by extension, any mental energy we expend worrying over these things is also in vain because in worrying, we've left God out of the picture.

So include God in all you do. Make sure He is behind you 100 percent. Hand over your worries to Him. . . . Those efforts won't be in vain.

---

*Unless You are with me, Lord, I can do nothing.
Help me look to You in everything. Amen.*

Sing His Praises

The Lord is my strength and my safe cover. My heart trusts in Him, and I am helped. So my heart is full of joy. I will thank Him with my song.
PSALM 28:7 NLV

Travel around the world and one of the things you'll find in common is singing. Yes, the music styles vary, the instruments may be unique, and the languages are different, but it's singing all the same. And even when we don't understand the words, singing still speaks to us, still communicates emotion.

Sometimes singing seems the only way to tell God how much we appreciate Him. Small wonder that Christians across the world and the centuries have praised God through song. And it doesn't matter whether you're a songbird or prefer singing silently in your heart. God hears.

Has your heart been lifted from worries? Lift up a song of thanks to God above.

Lord, I sing to You with joy and thanks. Amen.

It's Yours

"Do not worry about the things that belong to you.
For the best of all the land of Egypt is yours."
GENESIS 45:20 NLV

Joseph's brothers must have been dumbfounded. Joseph—this little brother they had discarded—was back in their lives, alive and well. And not only that—he offered them forgiveness and blessings. Then Pharaoh—ruler of mighty Egypt—opened his arms and his land to them too. They went from needy and undeserving and scared to "the best of all the land of Egypt is yours." Quite the change! But. . .God tops that. Pharaoh is nothing next to God, though we are certainly needy and undeserving and scared. And God's word to us is "Fear not. . . for it is [My] good pleasure to give you the kingdom" (Luke 12:32 ESV).

Do not worry about your stuff—your struggles either. For the best God has to give is yours.

Lord, what's Yours is mine. I am so amazed
and so grateful. So assured. Amen.

Note to Self

Truly my soul finds rest in God; my salvation
comes from him. . . . Yes, my soul, find rest
in God; my hope comes from him.
PSALM 62:1, 5 NIV

We may know as surely as we know our name or the color of our eyes that God is our salvation. That He is the One who is ever present with us, who is ever willing and ever ready to save us from hell, our troubles, and even ourselves. We may know that with Him is hope—certain hope, constant hope, absolute hope. But sometimes that knowledge doesn't make it soul deep. Sometimes we need to remind our souls what our heads know. Like the psalmist, we affirm, "Truly my soul finds rest in God." Then we have to address our souls: "Yes, my soul, find rest in God."

Feeling restless today? Talk to God—and to yourself too.

I find my rest in You, Lord. Yes, my soul,
find your rest in the Lord. Amen.

Good to Us

Return to your rest, O my soul.
For the Lord has been good to you.
PSALM 116:7 NLV

Need another soul talk? This time the psalmist tells his soul to leave anxiety behind and return to rest, to recall how good the Lord has been.

As worrisome things collect around us, they begin to block our view of God's goodness. One worry sprouts at our feet like a weed. Then other worries pop up next to the first worry. The worries grow taller, and if we let them, they morph into briars.

But if we tell our souls, "Rest—for God has been good to you," if we turn over in our minds the good things that come from the Lord. . .the briars are razed, the weeds crushed. And we see unobstructed God's goodness that ever surrounds us.

Lord, You have been so very good to me. Help my worries disappear in view of Your goodness. Amen.

Anxious but Not. . .

*But we have this treasure in jars of clay to show
that this all-surpassing power is from God and not
from us. We are hard pressed on every side, but not
crushed; perplexed, but not in despair; persecuted,
but not abandoned; struck down, but not destroyed.*

2 CORINTHIANS 4:7–9 NIV

Jars of clay. Plain. Rough around the edges. Prone to breaking.
That certainly describes us. (Though we may try to be less
plain!) Yet in Bible logic, being a "jar of clay" is a beautiful
thing—a condition that highlights the treasure of God in us.
And although we are fragile creations, we are strengthened
by God's power. Worries may bring us low for a time, but
we will not remain down. Anxiety may strain us, but we will
not snap. What a promise! What peace of mind and heart.

---

*Lord, I feel so vulnerable, but I know that
You are with me, Your Spirit within
me, keeping me whole. Amen.*

Rest Awaits

And it shall come to pass in the day that the
LORD shall give thee rest from thy sorrow, and
from thy fear, and from the hard bondage
wherein thou wast made to serve.
ISAIAH 14:3 KJV

Isaiah prophesied a day when God would give His people rest.
In the days of captivity, they could look forward with hope.

Difficult times, stressful times may seem to us like some
sort of cruel bondage that will continue forever. But as God's
beloved, we are not destined for sorrow and fear and hard
bondage. God has the opposite in mind. "And after you have
suffered a little while, the God of all grace, who has called
you to his eternal glory in Christ, will himself restore, con-
firm, strengthen, and establish you" (1 Peter 5:10 ESV). That
day will come. Look forward without anxiety but with hope.

Lord, please fill me with patience and
trust, strength and hope until these days
of worry give way to days of rest. Amen.

When High Meets Lowly

For this is what the high and exalted One says—he who lives forever, whose name is holy: "I live in a high and holy place, but also with the one who is contrite and lowly in spirit, to revive the spirit of the lowly and to revive the heart of the contrite."

ISAIAH 57:15 NIV

It doesn't matter what we've been through or done. We don't ever have to be anxious about approaching God. As long as our hearts are humble before Him, He meets us in the low places. The places where we've stumbled. The places where we've all but given up. The places where we can't see. The places where worries, fear, or doubt are unwanted companions. In fact, God says He does more than meet us there. He lives with the lowly to revive us, heart and spirit.

Lord, I'm bowing before You today with every shortcoming laid before You. How I need revival. How wonderful You are to revive me! Amen.

Written to Be Read

Everything that was written in the past was
written to teach us, so that through the endurance
taught in the Scriptures and the encouragement
they provide we might have hope.
ROMANS 15:4 NIV

The Bible is the definitive handbook for godly living. . .and a whole lot more. The verses show us right and wrong, yes. They also spur us on. Throughout scripture we see examples of endurance—faith in action in all kinds of turbulence. And we're encouraged so we can navigate the turbulence ourselves. Everything that was written was written for us—for our benefit.

It's simple enough to claim the benefits. Just read God's Word. Don't just plan on reading it or just leaf through once in a while. Read it regularly. And as you read, God will show your heart how to endure, how to be encouraged, how to have hope.

Lord, scripture is a precious resource. Help
me treasure it. Help me learn what I need
to learn for the anxious days. Amen.

Lord of All

In that day the LORD will whistle for the fly that is at the end of the streams of Egypt, and for the bee that is in the land of Assyria. And they will all come.

ISAIAH 7:18–19 ESV

We don't have to worry when the Lord is our God. He is too powerful of an ally. So instead of dwelling on a worry, we can pick a passage of scripture that illustrates God's omnipotence and dwell on that. A passage like Isaiah 7:18–19.

Have you ever tried ordering a fly or a bee around? *Uh, no.* They zip here, there. . .wherever they want. But God's whistle is their command. With just a sound, they will come. God is able to control the vastness of the universe as well as the tiniest detail.

He can even calm our unruly hearts with a whisper.

Lord, whatever I'm facing, You're still God, my God, and Master over anything that worries me. Amen.

Treasured Thoughts

*But Mary treasured up all these things
and pondered them in her heart.*

LUKE 2:19 NIV

Baby Jesus was only hours old, and His first visitors—a ragtag group of shepherds straight from the field—arrived. They spoke of the angel's glorious message, and amazement filled anyone who heard. We might imagine them exclaiming at the news, wide-eyed and energized. *But Mary. . .Mary* took the words and treasured them in her heart. She pondered the grand thing this tiny infant would do.

Ours is an out-loud world. We often process what's unfolding in our lives by talking things over, by sharing—and there's nothing wrong with that. Yet sometimes what we need most is reflection. Quiet times between us and the Word. Quiet moments when God speaks to us and makes sense of the unexpected, the astonishing, and—yes—the worrying.

*Quiet me, Lord. Help me see things through Your eyes as
I sit here with You, as I think about Your words. Amen.*

A Nighttime Meditation

My eyes stay open through the watches of the night, that I may meditate on your promises.
PSALM 119:148 NIV

It's two in the morning. You should be sleeping. Should be but aren't because you're staring at the ceiling. What's keeping your eyes open? Worries. Thoughts about the day gone by and the days ahead. An anxious rumination.

The psalmist didn't write of nights spent fast asleep. "I stay awake through the night, thinking about your promise," he said (Psalm 119:148 NLT). He was so captivated by God's Word that it was the meditation of his heart at night—and all day (see v. 97).

Many times, anxious nights are just a continuation of anxious days. But we can get ready for peaceful nighttimes by soaking up scripture in the daylight. Then may our sleepless nights not be because of worries but because we don't want to stop thinking about God's words!

Lord, I love Your Word! Help it become my meditation whether it's morning or evening or midnight. Amen.

Worry-Proof Love

*I am convinced that nothing can ever separate
us from God's love. Neither death nor life, neither
angels nor demons, neither our fears for today
nor our worries about tomorrow—not even the
powers of hell can separate us from God's love.*
ROMANS 8:38 NLT

More constant than the rising and setting of the sun. More fixed than ancient mountains. More life-giving than the air in our lungs and the blood in our veins. Deeper than the deep blue sea. Closer than a heartbeat. Stronger than the strongest metal, the hardest diamond. More unfathomable than the universe yet nearer and dearer than a loved one's embrace. More powerful than hell. More enduring than eternity.

And far, far greater than our fears and worries. . . That's God's love. A love that is with us through anything because nothing can separate us from Love Himself. He simply won't let it.

---

*Lord, help me see You and Your love above
all, fears and worries included! Amen.*

Undivided

Come close to God, and God will come close to you.
Wash your hands, you sinners; purify your hearts, for
your loyalty is divided between God and the world.

JAMES 4:8 NLT

God loves us dearly. And like a husband who becomes jealous when his wife's affection strays, God becomes jealous when our faithfulness to Him isn't so faithful. We can't split fidelity. We can't be devoted to Him plus another and still call it devotion. Paul warned the Corinthians, "You cannot have a part in both the Lord's table and the table of demons. Are we trying to arouse the Lord's jealousy?" (1 Corinthians 10:21–22 NIV).

But could it be that we feel this division too? Not as jealousy. As unease. We know where our hearts belong. When they aren't there—close to God—we can't be at ease. So the Bible says to come clean. To come close. And the God who still loves us dearly will come close to us.

Lord, forgive me. Come close to me. Amen.

Bear with Them

*Be completely humble and gentle; be
patient, bearing with one another in love.*
EPHESIANS 4:2 NIV

A coworker sits in the cubicle next to yours, anxiously tapping her pen on the desk. Your sister is eating lunch with you; you can tell something is on her mind, but it isn't the conversation. The cashier is clearly stressed and distracted and consequently mistake-prone. A friend is so worried about something in her life that you don't seem to exist to her anymore. You can't get anywhere near another friend for fear that she'll snap your head off.

We know how anxiety affects us—how it can make us fidgety, preoccupied, sometimes nasty messes. So when we recognize the telltale signs in others, we should be the first to offer grace. Let's remember how patient and understanding the Lord is to us in our worries. And let's be His reflection to others in theirs.

*Lord, help me reach out to other people with
the grace and peace You've given me. Amen.*

Peacefully Ever After

God shall wipe away all tears from their eyes;
and there shall be no more death, neither sorrow,
nor crying, neither shall there be any more pain:
for the former things are passed away. And he that
sat upon the throne said, Behold, I make all things new.
REVELATION 21:4-5 KJV

It sounds like the ending to a fairy tale, along the lines of "And they lived happily ever after." Once God has vanquished evil, He will transform the old, ravaged world into a new, shining world. He will form a new heaven and a new earth, where living happily, peacefully ever after is the ending of our stories—and is actually the beginning of our never-ending stories. Stories without tears because God will wipe them away. Stories without death or sorrow, crying or pain. And stories without worry. *There will be no more anxiety.* Think of that!

Lord, one day I won't have to imagine what perfect peace
is like. I will know. Thank You for this promise. Amen.

Gains from Pains

For our light affliction, which is but for
a moment, worketh for us a far more
exceeding and eternal weight of glory.
2 CORINTHIANS 4:17 KJV

"No pain, no gain" may not be our favorite expression to hear, but we all know that rough things can lead to rewards. The breaking down of muscles leads to strength. The pain of childbirth leads to motherhood. The tough conversation leads to healing. . . . "The little troubles we suffer now for a short time are making us ready for the great things God is going to give us forever" (2 Corinthians 4:17 NLV). The things we don't want to go through can lead where we want to go. This may not feel true, but our troubles really are for a short time. And they really are preparing us for glorious gains. God has taken great pains to ensure that they will.

Lord, help me stay calm and strong through
the things that trouble me. They'll be
nothing next to eternal glory! Amen.

169

Growing Dependence

The troubles of my heart have grown.
Bring me out of my suffering.
PSALM 25:17 NLV

Maybe the worries have piled up like dirty dishes in a sink. Maybe the stresses have multiplied like interest on a credit card. Maybe the troubles of your heart have grown, as they did for the psalm writer, and are still growing. You're ready to cry uncle. "Bring me out of my suffering. . . . Keep me safe, Lord, and set me free" sounds exactly like your heart's prayer (vv. 17, 20 NLV).

Though we don't know how or how long until God will change our circumstances, our cries to Him are never wasted breath. Sometimes the silver lining of anxiety is that it draws us continually back to God's side. We learn our need for Him in our worries. . .which carries over into our days even when the worries themselves have passed.

Lord, thank You for using everything in my life
to deepen my relationship with You. Amen.

Through the Troubles

Many are the afflictions of the righteous,
but the LORD delivers him out of them all. He
keeps all his bones; not one of them is broken.
PSALM 34:19–20 ESV

We may wish for divine immunity from troubles. However, scripture doesn't say that nothing will ever happen to those who believe in the Lord Jesus. Just the opposite. "Many are the afflictions of the righteous," Psalm 34:19 says.

So what can we make of the second half of verse 19 and then verse 20? "The LORD delivers him out of them all. He keeps all his bones; not one of them is broken." Experience tells us that we're not always removed from our afflictions and never hurt by them. Perhaps to understand, we need to see the contrast in the next verse—"Affliction will slay the wicked" (v. 21 ESV). In affliction, the wicked will be brought down, but we will be brought through.

Lord, preserve me through these
troubles. Perfect me in them. Amen.

The Other Kind of Anxious

*You won't spend the rest of your lives
chasing your own desires, but you will
be anxious to do the will of God.*

1 PETER 4:2 NLT

Is there a good kind of anxious? Yes, though of course it's not the anxious that makes us unable to rest because we're anticipating something. It's anxiousness that makes us strive toward something.

Christ redeemed our lives, and we don't live the same way we did when we were bound by sin. Peter wrote, "You won't spend the rest of your lives chasing your own desires." A new desire has usurped sin: an anxiousness to do God's will. And being anxious to do God's will is wholly unlike the anxiety that leaves us uneasy and fearful, because every step we take in living for God keeps us in step with the One who is our peace.

*Lord, may my only anxiousness be the good kind—
the kind that leaves me eager to do Your will. Amen.*

More Than Halfway

GOD met me more than halfway,
he freed me from my anxious fears.

PSALM 34:4 MSG

The prodigal son was heading home. He had messed up his life, but now he had made up his mind to go back to his father. Nerves ajangle, speech at the ready, no doubt he was filled with anxious thoughts about his reception and his fate. But he was still a long way off when his father ran out to meet him. (Luke 15:11-21.)

God meets us when we return to Him in repentance. God also meets us in every fear, and He meets us more than halfway. When we've just begun to take our first step into His presence—have just said our first words in prayer—He is already there. With open arms. With lavish love. With freedom from our anxious fears.

Lord, You see my need before I know my
need. Thank You for meeting me here. Amen.

More with Us

"Don't be afraid," the prophet answered. "Those who are with us are more than those who are with them."

2 KINGS 6:16 NIV

Elisha's servant awoke to find an enemy army surrounding his city, and alas, the horses and chariots didn't disappear when he rubbed his sleepy eyes. Suddenly, he was fearful; he was worried. *What are we going to do?!*

We might ask ourselves that same question when we're suddenly fearful and worried about something confronting us. To our eyes, we're outnumbered. Importantly, one of the first things Elisha did was pray—not for deliverance but for his servant's eyes to be opened to see God's protection that was already surrounding them (2 Kings 6:17). God's ways of aiding us are supernatural and unsearchable. He may not reveal legions of angels when we pray, but He will open our hearts to see that He is with us and greater than any number of foes.

Lord, help me see that I am not alone in these worries. Amen.

Worry about the Holy

"Don't fear what they fear. Don't take on their worries.
If you're going to worry, worry about The Holy. Fear
GOD-of-the-Angel-Armies. The Holy can be either
a Hiding Place or a Boulder blocking your way."
ISAIAH 8:12–14 MSG

The Lord's words of caution fit right in with modern times: "Do not call conspiracy everything this people calls a conspiracy; do not fear what they fear, and do not dread it" (Isaiah 8:12 NIV). If we believe every "the sky is falling" article or post, there's no end to things to be wary of. But God's Word tells us that rather than placing too much emphasis on those worries, we are to focus our attention on God. We should fear Him.

And that fear isn't a hindrance to us. It actually helps us as we face all the other fears.

Lord, teach me to live in fear—in awe, in reverence—of You
so I can live without fearing what others fear. Amen.

No Judgment-Day Worries

*So we have come to know and to believe the love
that God has for us. God is love, and whoever
abides in love abides in God, and God abides in
him. By this is love perfected with us, so that we
may have confidence for the day of judgment,
because as he is so also are we in this world.*

1 JOHN 4:16–17 ESV

Judgment day. If we had to earn our way into heaven by
our own merits, we might feel uncertain thinking about the
coming judgment day—we might be downright worried. But
God's love made forgiveness possible, and forgiveness made
us right with God. Each of us no longer stands on our own
two feet as we stand before God. Jesus, the One in whose
footsteps we follow, has stood in for us. He enables us to
stand. And through Him we have confidence for that day!

---

*Lord, thank You for Your love that
casts out fear (see 1 John 4:18). Amen.*

In Great Vexations

Hannah answered, "No, my lord, I am a woman troubled in spirit. I have drunk neither wine nor strong drink, but I have been pouring out my soul before the LORD. . . . All along I have been speaking out of my great anxiety and vexation."
1 SAMUEL 1:15–16 ESV

Hannah had a loving husband, but Hannah had no children, and that was a huge deal. Having children was so important in Hannah's culture and to her personally. Her soul cried out for a son. One day at the temple, her silent, intense praying attracted the attention of the priest, Eli—because he thought she was drunk!

Unlike people, God doesn't recoil when He hears our tear-soaked prayers, and He never misunderstands. He listens. And He answers—often in exactly the way we hope. He certainly did for Hannah.

Lord, You welcome my prayers however I'm feeling. I can pour out my heart to You. Thank You for listening, for understanding, for answering. Amen.

Praise Anyway

"When I expected good, then trouble came.
When I waited for light, darkness came.
My heart is troubled and does not rest.
Days of trouble are before me."
JOB 30:26–27 NLV

Job's life had been wonderful. Then it was terrible. Although we probably haven't experienced the depth of Job's troubles, we can relate to his words. Trouble, darkness, can come when we least expect it. And when it's here, it seems it's here to stay.

Satan tried to prove that Job's faith depended on his circumstances. But Job's faith depended on God. Job trusted God come trouble or good, darkness or light: "The Lord gave and the Lord has taken away. Praise the name of the Lord" (Job 1:21 NLV). God *is* trustworthy even when we don't understand our troubles. God *is* faithful even when we can't see the end of those troubles. The question is whether we'll praise God despite them.

Lord, I'm struggling right now, but I choose to
accept Your will and praise You anyway. Amen.

Why So Troubled?

The angel of God called to Hagar from heaven, and said, "Why are you so troubled, Hagar? Do not be afraid."

GENESIS 21:17 NLV

God's question to Hagar might seem laughable. Why was she so troubled? From Hagar's perspective, how much worse could it get? Kicked out of her home. Wandering in the desert. Afraid she and her son would die of thirst. . . But *still* God asked, "Why are you so troubled?" He told her, "Do not be afraid"—because He'd never stopped looking out for them. He okayed Abraham's sending the pair away. He heard Ishmael's cry. He planned to make Ishmael into a great nation. And in the meantime, He quenched Hagar's physical thirst with water from a well even as He revived her faith.

It's not so difficult to imagine God calling to us, "Why are you so troubled? Do not be afraid."

Lord, help me look beyond my troubles to You saying, "Do not be afraid." Amen.

Shepherded

*The false gods say what is not true. . . . Their comfort
means nothing. So the people go from place to place like
sheep and are troubled because they have no shepherd.*
ZECHARIAH 10:2 NLV

Zechariah described people who did not follow God. Their
idols were no help, no shepherd, and the people were aimless
and troubled. Centuries later, Jesus witnessed the same thing:
"As He saw many people, He had loving-pity on them. They
were troubled and were walking around everywhere. They
were like sheep without a shepherd" (Matthew 9:36 NLV).

For unbelievers, nothing has changed. They are still lost
and troubled. They haven't yet met Jesus: The One who has
compassion when He sees us "harassed and helpless" (Matthew 9:36 NIV). The One who leads us to peaceful meadows.
The One who carries us on His shoulders. The One who is
our Shepherd.

Pass the Word on!

---

*Thank You for shepherding me, Lord.
Use me to call others to You. Amen.*

Just Stay Calm

"The Lord himself will fight for you. Just stay calm."
Exodus 14:14 nlt

After a lengthy bout of plagues, Pharaoh let God's people leave Egypt. But not long after that, he had a change of heart and tracked down the ex-slaves. Moses and the Israelites were trapped with Egypt's military might on one side, the Red Sea on the other. And in all that chaos and alarm, the Israelites forgot who was on *their* side.

Moses' command—"Just stay calm"—would have been absurd without the reminder that "the Lord himself will fight for you." The Lord Himself fights on His people's behalf—then and now. His command remains "Be still, and know that I am God" (Psalm 46:10 niv). Whatever difficult situations we're stuck between, we can trust our God to be smack-dab in the middle with us and for us.

Lord, true calmness is impossible without knowing You. Help me know that You are God so that I can just stay calm. Amen.

Let Us

Let us not sleep, as the rest do, but let us keep wide awake (alert, watchful, cautious, and on our guard) and let us be sober (calm, collected, and circumspect).

1 THESSALONIANS 5:6 AMPC

Jesus will return. The date is unknown to us, but the fact is certain. So Paul had two-part advice for Christians: Keep awake. Be sober.

"Let us keep wide awake (alert, watchful, cautious, and on our guard)." It's easy for life as it is to lull us into thinking life will always be as it is. It's even easier to let this life prevent us from living in ready anticipation of the Lord's return. Yet keeping awake doesn't mean facing each day with eyes frantically scanning our surroundings. "Let us be sober (calm, collected, and circumspect)." We can be alert *and* calm simultaneously. Watchful but not worried. Cautious but not anxious. On our guard but not on edge. . . . Let's begin this very day.

No more sleepwalking for me, Lord.
Help me keep awake and calm. Amen.

Leaning on the Lord

*Be still and rest in the Lord; wait for Him
and patiently lean yourself upon Him.*
PSALM 37:7 AMPC

Sometimes we need someone to lean on. To strengthen, to support, to comfort us. Like the runner who collapses and her teammates help her to her feet and to the finish line. The child who falls asleep resting against Mom's side. The wife who cries on her husband's shoulder. . . . Psalm 37:7 talks about leaning, only this time we're leaning on God.

If we think of God as a being hovering far above us, it might seem strange to imagine leaning on Him. While God is spirit, He also became flesh. Jesus was a man with arms to support, shoulders to cry on. And although He is not physically with us now, His presence is still just as real. On your anxious days, lean yourself on Him.

Lord, my heart is restless. Help me be still, help me wait, as I lean my whole self upon You. Amen.

Wings to Rest

*Fear and trembling overwhelm me, and I can't
stop shaking. Oh, that I had wings like a dove;
then I would fly away and rest! I would fly
far away to the quiet of the wilderness.*

PSALM 55:5–7 NLT

Oh to fly away! How many times have we longed to escape our anxieties? To be able to leave worry behind in the careworn jumble that is life sometimes and to land again somewhere quiet, someplace where we can rest and recharge. That might be a daydream, but God does promise us wings. Not wings to fly away from trouble. Wings to fly above it. "Those who hope in the LORD will renew their strength. They will soar on wings like eagles" (Isaiah 40:31 NIV).

And when anxiety temporarily clips our wings? Then we rest beneath *His* wings (Psalm 17:8).

---

*Lord, I want to fly away, but I will hope
in You, right here in the worries. Give me
fresh strength. Give me rest, I pray. Amen.*

God's Way

*When Pharaoh let the people go, God did not
lead them on the road through the Philistine
country, though that was shorter. For God said,
"If they face war, they might change their minds
and return to Egypt." So God led the people
around by the desert road toward the Red Sea.*

EXODUS 13:17–18 NIV

God could have taken the people away from Egypt by a shorter route. He chose not to. He led them the long way around. He even led them toward a watery obstacle called the Red Sea.

Our lives may appear to be a series of detours and delays. At least, they appear so to us. But what the Israelites couldn't see and we can't see either are the dangers we would have encountered had we gone the shorter way. From God's point of view, that winding way will take us straight to where we need to be.

---

*Lord, this isn't the path I would choose. But
I trust Your choice, Your purpose. Amen.*

Trust, and Trust Some More

Cause me to hear thy lovingkindness in the morning; for in thee do I trust: cause me to know the way wherein I should walk; for I lift up my soul unto thee. . . . Teach me to do thy will; for thou art my God: thy spirit is good.

PSALM 143:8, 10 KJV

A fisherman who trusts the watertightness of his boat is not worried that it will sink. A baby who trusts her parent to hold her is not uneasy as she sleeps. A hiker who trusts the map is not concerned about getting lost.

And a woman who trusts God is not anxious. That level of trust isn't instant. Many times we're imperfectly trusting. But with each sunrise, we can renew our trust. We can entrust our souls, ourselves, to God. We can loosen our grip of control, take hold of His hand—and let our anxious hearts rest assured.

Lord, every day and in every worry,
I will keep on trusting You. Amen.

Index

NEW TESTAMENT

About the Author

Linda Hang is a freelance writer and editor. She enjoys old movies, kayaking, and discovering each day what God has planned for her.